Echoes of Elders

Wisdom from my African Ancestors

Mark Irabor

ISBN: 979-8-9897932-2-8 (Paperback)
ISBN: 979-8-9897932-3-5 (e-book – EPUB)

Library of Congress Control Number: 2024910598

MarkJoy Publishing LLC
P. O. BOX 73741
Houston, TX 77273

Publisher's Cataloging-in-Publication data
Names: Irabor, Mark, author.
Title: Echoes of elders: wisdom from my African ancestors / Mark Irabor.
Description: Houston, TX: MarkJoy Publishing LLC, 2024.
Identifiers: LCCN: 2024910598 | ISBN: 979-8-9897932-2-8 (paperback) | 979-8-9897932-3-5 (ebook)
Subjects: LCSH Proverbs, African. | Folklore--Africa. | Fables, African. | Tales--Africa. | BISAC FICTION / Fairy Tales, Folk Tales, Legends & Mythology | FICTION / World Literature / Africa / General | BODY, MIND & SPIRIT / Inspiration & Personal Growth
Classification: LCC BL2400 I73 2024 | DDC 398.20967--dc23

Dedication

I dedicate this book to our African ancestors, who have played a crucial role in preserving our rich African culture and passing down their wisdom to future generations. Your teachings and values continue to resonate in the hearts and minds of those who have come after you. We are reminded of the invaluable lessons you have taught us – lessons of unity, resilience, and the importance of embracing our cultural identity. Your legacy lives on through us as we carry forward our traditions and pass on their wisdom to future generations.

Our African ancestors have faced countless challenges and hardships, yet they remained resilient and steadfast in upholding our traditions and beliefs. Their perseverance and strength have shaped who we are today and continue to guide us as we navigate through life.

Through their stories and wisdom, our ancestors have instilled a sense of pride in our heritage and a deep appreciation for their sacrifices to ensure that our culture lives on. Their voices may have been silenced by time, but their words still echo in our hearts, constantly reminding us of the importance of preserving our African roots.

Mark Irabor

We express our deepest gratitude to our African ancestors for your shared wisdom and knowledge. Your legacy will forever be etched in our hearts, serving as a guiding light as we strive for a brighter future.

Thank you for your enduring legacy and for ensuring that our African culture remains a source of strength and inspiration for future generations.

Table of Contents

Echoes of Elders

Stealth and Strength

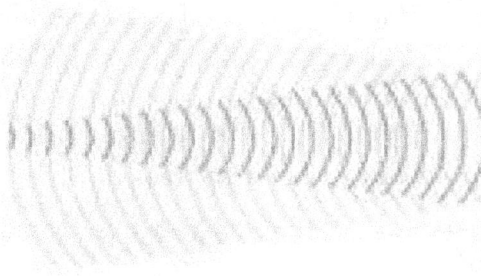

"The slow approach of a tiger is not
an indication of its weakness."
-Nigerian Proverb.

In the vast expanse of the wilderness, where the rhythms of nature play out in an intricate dance, the tiger reigns as one of the most formidable predators. Its sleek, powerful form and piercing gaze evoke a sense of awe and fear in those who encounter it. Yet, there is more to this majestic creature than meets the eye. Contrary to common belief, a tiger's slow approach does not indicate its weakness; rather, it is a testament to its strategic prowess and unwavering patience.

Picture a scene in the dense foliage of a tropical forest, where the air is thick with humidity, and the scent of foliage hangs heavy. A tiger, adorned with striking orange and black stripes, moves with deliberate slowness through the undergrowth. Every movement is calculated, and each step is taken with a sense of purpose. To the untrained eye, this deliberate pace may seem incongruent with the ferocious reputation of the tiger. However, to those who understand the ways of the wild, it is a display of mastery.

In the world of the tiger, patience is not merely a virtue; it is a survival strategy honed through centuries of evolution. Unlike other predators that rely on speed and agility to pursue their prey, the tiger employs a different approach. It understands that the key to a successful hunt lies not in impulsive action but in careful observation and calculated anticipation.

As the tiger stalks its prey, its slow and methodical movements serve multiple purposes. First, they allow the tiger to blend seamlessly into its surroundings, effectively becoming one with the environment. The dappled sunlight filters through the shade above, casting shifting patterns of light and shadow upon the forest floor. The tiger moves with the fluidity of a shadow, its striped coat providing perfect camouflage amidst the foliage.

Secondly, the slow approach of the tiger serves to lull its prey into a false sense of security. To an unsuspecting deer grazing in the clearing, the tiger may appear as little more than a trick of the light or a fleeting glimpse of movement in the underbrush. Its gradual advancement is imperceptible, each step taken with such stealth that the prey remains unaware of the imminent danger lurking nearby.

However, in the final moments of the hunt, the true strength of the tiger's patience is revealed. As it draws closer to its quarry, the tiger enters a heightened focus and intensity state. Every muscle in its body tenses with anticipation, ready to unleash its full power in a burst of speed and precision.

In a single explosive moment, the tiger pounces with a primal roar that reverberates through the forest. Its prey, caught off guard by the sudden onslaught, has little chance of escape. With jaws like steel traps and claws like razors, the tiger dispatches its quarry with ruthless efficiency. Yet, amidst the chaos of the hunt, there is a profound sense of harmony and balance. The tiger does not kill for the sake of killing, nor does it take more than it needs to sustain itself. It is a predator guided by instinct and necessity; the natural order of the wilderness dictates its actions.

In the grand tapestry of life, the slow approach of a tiger serves as a poignant reminder of the power of patience and the wisdom of restraint. It teaches us that true strength is not measured by brute force or aggression but by the ability to wait, observe, and strike precisely when the time is right.

Beyond the realm of the jungle, the lesson of the tiger resonates deeply in our lives. In a world that often values speed and instant gratification, we would do well to heed the wisdom of the tiger. Whether pursuing our goals, navigating challenges, or interacting with others, there is strength to be found in the slow, deliberate approach. Like the tiger, we must learn to move with purpose and intention, cultivating patience as a character's cornerstone. Through patience, we gain clarity, resilience, and the ability to seize opportunities when they arise. Through patience, we harness the power of restraint, avoiding impulsive actions that may lead to regret or downfall.

In the end, the slow approach of a tiger is not a sign of weakness but of strength tempered by wisdom. It is a reminder that sometimes, the greatest victories are won not through force but through patience, perseverance, and unwavering determination.

Echoes of Elders

In the late 1980s, the parable unfolded before me, casting its profound wisdom on the art of decision-making. During this time, an investment brokerage firm manager extended an enticing invitation for me to join their ranks as a financial analyst. Amidst the enticing allure of the comprehensive benefits package he detailed, I paused to reflect upon his proposition's weight.

As our conversation unfolded, punctuated by his persuasive pitch for why I should choose his company over its competitors, my mind swirled with excitement at the prospect. Yet, in a serendipitous moment, my gaze drifted downwards, landing upon his shoes. To my surprise, I beheld a conspicuous flaw – a gaping hole adorning his right shoe. In that instant, a profound realization washed over me, prompting a crucial revelation about the nature of decision-making.

The sight of that humble imperfection, nestled inconspicuously amidst the grandeur of our discussion, served as an unexpected catalyst for introspection. It compelled me to halt in my tracks, urging me to reassess the pace at which I approached the crossroads of opportunity and choice. In that fleeting moment, I came to understand that therein lies the essence of wisdom – not merely in the swiftness of our decisions but in the deliberate and strategic approach we employ, even if it means progressing at a more measured pace.

In the wake of this revelatory encounter, I was confronted with a profound truth: the journey towards informed decision-making is not a race to be won hastily but rather a meticulous exploration of options guided by prudence and discernment. It is a journey marked by the artful navigation of uncertainties and complexities, wherein the virtues of patience and thoughtful consideration reign supreme.

Too often, in the relentless pursuit of progress and success, we find ourselves trapped in the trappings of haste, heedless of the invaluable insights that await those who dare to pause and reflect. Amidst the quietude of contemplation, the nuances of our choices come into sharp focus, revealing hidden depths and unforeseen consequences that elude the hurried eye.

In decision-making, speed is not synonymous with efficacy; instead, the measured cadence of our deliberations yields the most enduring outcomes. Like a master strategist surveying the terrain before engaging in battle, we must carefully approach each decision, weighing the risks and rewards with a discerning eye.

Indeed, in the art of slowing down, we discover the true essence of strength—not in the impulsive rush towards a predetermined destination but in the deliberate strides we take, guided by foresight and prudence. In a world where haste is often exalted as a virtue, the steadfast resolve to pause, reflect, and chart a course with clarity and purpose distinguishes the wise from the reckless.

As I stood at the precipice of choice, confronted by the subtle yet profound lesson embodied in that worn shoe, I realized that true wisdom lies not in the swiftness of our actions but in the thoughtful intentionality with which we approach each decision. It is a lesson that has reverberated through time, guiding my steps ever since and imbuing my journey with a newfound sense of purpose and clarity.

In life, decisions are the threads that weave together the fabric of our existence, shaping the course of our journey in ways both seen and unseen. And it is in the art of slowing down, in embracing the serenity of contemplation, that we unlock the boundless potential inherent within each choice.

Thus, let us heed the wisdom of the ages and embrace the art of slowing down in our pursuit of greatness, for it is in the deliberate pause, in the measured stride, that we discover the true essence of strength and resilience. And it is in the stillness of reflection that we unearth the treasures of wisdom that lie dormant within us, waiting to be unearthed by those with the courage to slow down and listen.

Twine of Tradition

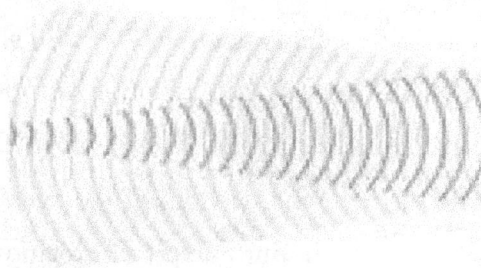

"A palm wine tapper must make the tapping rope his best companion."
-African Proverb

This proverb originates from African culture, particularly among communities where palm wine tapping is a common practice. Palm wine tapping involves extracting sap from various species of palm trees, which is then fermented to produce a traditional alcoholic beverage.

Palm wine tapping is often viewed as a symbiotic relationship between the tapper and the palm tree. The tapper relies on the tree for its sap, while the tree benefits from the tapper's care in ensuring sustainable tapping practices. By making the tapping rope their best companion, the tapper respects the natural resources they depend on and recognizes the importance of nurturing and preserving them.

In Nigerian cultures, palm wine tapping is not just a livelihood but a cultural tradition passed down through generations. By valuing the tapping rope as their best companion, the tapper honors the knowledge and techniques handed down by their ancestors. Additionally, the phrase highlights the communal aspect of palm wine tapping, where tappers form close bonds with their tools and fellow tappers, sharing experiences and expertise.

Overall, this proverb underscores themes of skill, respect for nature, and community within the context of palm wine tapping, offering insights into the values and practices of the culture where it originates.

The incident involving the investment brokerage manager mentioned in the last chapter, attempting to entice

17

me into joining his firm, serves as a poignant example of the nuanced art of persuasion within the realm of professional endeavors. The manager sought to allure me with promises of lucrative financial benefits, accompanied by the assertion that I would be capable of earning substantial sums on a monthly basis. He stated that I could earn thirty thousand dollars a month, which was a tremendous amount of money at that time. However, despite his earnest efforts, it became apparent that he lacked a fundamental understanding of the essential tools of persuasion inherent to his trade.

The incongruity of his approach was glaringly evident in his attire, specifically the presence of a conspicuous hole in his shoes. This seemingly minor detail spoke volumes about his disregard for the importance of professional presentation and the role it plays in cultivating a sense of credibility and trustworthiness. Indeed, his failure to recognize the significance of dressing appropriately as a foundational aspect of his professional image underscored a critical shortcoming in his understanding of the art of persuasion. I took one look at the hole in his shoe and shook my head.

In the context of his role as a recruiter for his firm, the importance of projecting an image of competence and professionalism cannot be overstated. By neglecting to prioritize his own presentation, he inadvertently undermined his credibility and detracted from the effectiveness of his persuasive efforts. The presence of the hole in his shoes symbolized a broader lack of attention to detail and professionalism, qualities that are paramount in the field of financial analysis. In a profession that hinges upon meticulous analysis and precision, the ability to demonstrate a keen eye for detail and a commitment to upholding high standards is essential. By showcasing a disregard for such fundamental principles, the manager failed to inspire confidence in his abilities and called into question the integrity and credibility of the firm he represented.

The disparity between his outward appearance and the promises he espoused regarding financial success further eroded his credibility as a persuasive communicator. While he sought to entice me with assurances of substantial monetary rewards, the incongruity of his presentation served as a stark reminder of the importance of authenticity and transparency in persuasive communication. Failing to align his words with his actions undermined the trust and credibility necessary to persuade others to join his firm effectively.

In reflecting on this encounter, it becomes evident that he lacked a comprehensive understanding of the tools of persuasion inherent to his trade. While he may have understood the financial incentives designed to attract potential recruits, he failed to recognize the importance of cultivating a professional image and projecting credibility and trustworthiness. In doing so, he inadvertently sabotaged his persuasive efforts and detracted from the effectiveness of his recruitment pitch. I knew I would not take the position because I lacked confidence in his pitch.

Ultimately, this incident serves as a sobering reminder of the multifaceted nature of persuasion within the realm of professional endeavors. Effective persuasion requires more than just the ability to articulate compelling arguments or offer enticing incentives; it necessitates a holistic understanding of the factors that influence human behavior and decision-making. By embracing the fundamental principles of professionalism, authenticity, and transparency, individuals can enhance their persuasive abilities and cultivate meaningful connections with others within their respective fields.

This proverb suggests that to excel in the craft of palm wine tapping, one must develop a close relationship with the tools of their trade. The "tapping rope" refers to the tool used to extract the sap from the palm tree. By considering this tool their "best companion," the tapper emphasizes the importance of skill and familiarity with their equipment.

Beneath the Surface

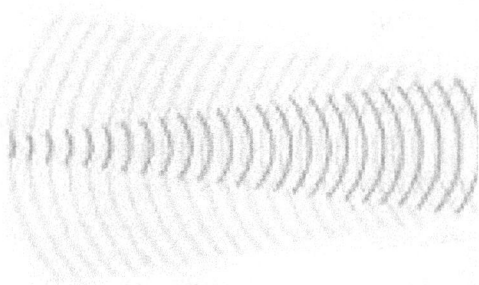

"My son, the soil is your friend
so learn to labor and to wait."
~Nigerian Proverb

The section of the quote "…learn to labor and to wait" is often attributed to Henry Wadsworth Longfellow, an American poet from the 19th century. This advice encapsulates the idea of combining hard work with patience and perseverance. Similarly, in Nigerian culture, a variation of this phrase, "My son, the soil is your friend, so learn to labor and to wait," is frequently used to impart wisdom.

This variation adds a layer of meaning by specifically referencing the soil as a friend to the son, highlighting the importance of respecting nature and cultivating a symbiotic relationship with the land. It explores the significance of these phrases in promoting a respectful and nurturing approach to working the land while emphasizing the values of hard work, patience, and perseverance in achieving success in agricultural endeavors.

The phrase "the soil is your friend" signifies a deep appreciation and respect for the natural world. Referring to the soil in this way encourages the son to recognize the value of the land as more than just a medium for planting. Instead, it emphasizes the importance of viewing the soil as a valuable ally in the cultivation process. This perspective highlights the interconnectedness between humans and the natural world, emphasizing the significance of nurturing and sustaining plant life through a symbiotic relationship with the soil.

Central to the phrase is the directive to "learn to labor and to wait." This emphasizes the importance of hard work, diligence, and perseverance. Cultivating the soil and tending to crops requires consistent effort over time and patience in waiting for the fruits of one's labor to flourish. This aspect of the advice underscores the value of dedication and commitment in achieving success in agricultural practices while acknowledging the need for patience and resilience in the face of challenges and setbacks.

In Nigerian culture, the phrase "My son, the soil is your friend, so learn to labor and to wait" is passed down through generations as a cultural or familial tradition. It highlights the significance of the son's connection to the land and the legacy of working the soil. This cultural perspective emphasizes the importance of stewardship and caretaking of the land for future generations, promoting a sense of responsibility toward preserving and nurturing the natural environment.

It is a reminder of the interconnectedness between humans and the natural world, particularly in the context of agriculture. It encourages a respectful and nurturing approach to working the land while emphasizing hard work, patience, and perseverance in achieving success. By recognizing the soil as a friend and understanding the importance of cultivating a symbiotic relationship with the land, individuals can develop a deeper appreciation for the natural world and contribute to sustainable agricultural practices that benefit both present and future generations.

Mark Irabor

This proverb conveys important lessons about the interconnectedness between humans and the natural world in the context of agriculture. They emphasize the significance of respecting nature, cultivating a symbiotic relationship with the soil, and embodying values such as hard work, patience, and perseverance in achieving success. By imparting these words of wisdom, individuals can develop a deeper appreciation for the land and contribute to sustainable agricultural practices that benefit themselves and the environment.

In our modern society, the proverb extends its relevance beyond agrarian contexts to resonate profoundly in the realms of business and career. Today, individuals often seek immediate gratification and success, neglecting the essential virtues of hard work, patience, and perseverance. This impatience manifests in a restless pursuit of instant rewards, leading many to abandon opportunities for growth and development.

In the year 2000, a notable instance of this scenario occurred during my professional tenure. At the time, I managed a childcare facility alongside my wife in New Orleans, and one of our employees, who served as a lead teacher, was on track for a significant promotion along with a considerable salary boost within three months. However, she unexpectedly approached me in my office, insisting on a raise within a week.

Echoes of Elders

Despite explaining that her salary review was scheduled for ninety days later and advising her to await the review process, she adamantly demanded an immediate salary increase. When I reiterated the importance of waiting for the review, she deemed my stance unacceptable and promptly resigned.

This impulsive decision stemmed from a pervasive societal mindset that prioritizes instant gratification over long-term investment. In the fast-paced world of work and business, individuals are often unwilling to endure the gradual process of advancement. Instead, they seek immediate validation and rewards, forsaking the invaluable lessons inherent in patience and perseverance.

The employee's resignation exemplifies the detrimental consequences of impatience in the professional sphere. Despite the promise of a lucrative promotion on the horizon, she chose to forfeit the opportunity in favor of immediate gain. This impulsive act deprived her of long-term career growth and underscored a fundamental lack of patience and foresight.

Six months later, the employee's abrupt departure came full circle as she reached out, seeking to reclaim her former position. However, her abrupt return underscored a stark realization: impatience begets regret. In her haste to secure instant gratification, she failed to recognize the enduring value of patience and perseverance. Now, faced with the consequences of her impulsive actions, she sought to rectify her decision and regain what she had hastily relinquished. She approached me, requesting the possibility of returning to her former role. Regrettably, our policy prohibited rehiring employees who resigned in the manner she did. Therefore, I declined to reemploy her.

This anecdote serves as a reminder of the timeless wisdom captured in the proverb, "Patience is a virtue." In today's fast-paced society, where instant gratification reigns supreme, cultivating patience and perseverance is more crucial than ever. Success in the professional sphere is not instantaneous; it requires dedication, resilience, and the willingness to endure challenges with unwavering patience.

The contemporary relevance of the proverb transcends traditional agrarian contexts to offer profound insights into the modern world of work and business. Impatience, driven by a desire for instant gratification, often leads individuals to forsake long-term opportunities for immediate rewards. However, as demonstrated by the employee's experience, impatience inevitably leads to regret, highlighting the importance of patience and perseverance in achieving sustainable success.

Roots of Sustenance

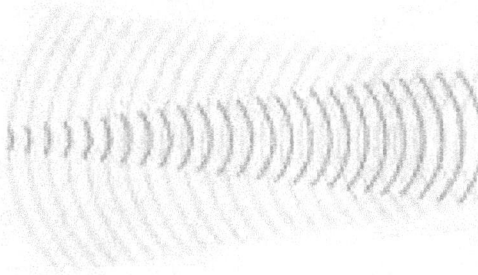

"To eat, a man must plant."
~Nigerian Proverb

As in the last chapter, this proverb encapsulates the fundamental concept of agriculture and sustenance. It emphasizes the reciprocal relationship between human beings and the land, highlighting the necessity of cultivation to obtain food and sustain life.

It emphasizes that individuals are responsible for contributing to their own sustenance by engaging in work activities. By planting and nurturing crops, people can ensure their own food security and reduce dependency on external sources. It recognizes that food production is not a passive process but requires active engagement with the land, acknowledging the role of environmental factors in agricultural success.

Implicit in the phrase is the idea of sustainability and stewardship of the land. By planting and cultivating crops, individuals are not only providing for their immediate needs but also contributing to the long-term health and productivity of the environment. This proverb conveys the importance of hard work, diligence, and patience in all our endeavors. It acknowledges that food production is labor-intensive and requires ongoing effort and perseverance.

In today's society, the age-old wisdom captured in the proverb "To eat, a man must plant" resonates deeply, transcending its agricultural origins to offer profound insights into contemporary life. This proverb sums up the fundamental concept of sustenance and underscores the reciprocal relationship between humanity and the environment, emphasizing the necessity of active engagement and responsibility in securing our basic needs.

During my college years, I juggled jobs as a security guard and a taxi cab driver to cover my tuition and rent. The demanding nature of driving often left me exhausted, collapsing onto the soft cushions of my small apartment at the day's end. Despite my fatigue, the whistle of hotel doormen hailing cabs for their guests echoed in my mind during moments of rest. This persistent sound served as a reminder that I needed to rise and work diligently to meet my financial obligations.

At its core, this proverb emphasizes the importance of self-sufficiency and resilience in the face of modern challenges. In an era marked by increasing reliance on external sources for sustenance and convenience, it serves as a powerful reminder of the value of self-reliance. By planting and nurturing crops, individuals ensure their own food security and reduce dependency on unsustainable food systems, promoting a more resilient and sustainable future.

It highlights the interconnectedness between human actions and the health of the planet, highlighting the need for sustainable practices in food production and land management. By cultivating crops responsibly, individuals contribute to their immediate needs and the long-term health and productivity of the environment, fostering a more harmonious relationship between humanity and nature.

During my college years as a security guard, I faced the harsh extremes of winter cold and relentless southern summer heat. There were moments when I hesitated to leave the comfort of my bed for work. However, the Nigerian proverb "to eat, a man must plant" echoed in my mind, serving as a reminder that I needed to persevere. On those reluctant days, I recalled the necessity of working to earn a living and put food on the table.

This proverb also implies the recognition of the value of hard work, diligence, and patience in achieving our goals. In a society characterized by instant gratification and quick fixes, it serves as a timely reminder of the enduring importance of perseverance and dedication in all our endeavors. Whether in agriculture or other aspects of life, success requires ongoing effort and commitment, and "To eat, a man must plant" summarizes this timeless truth.

This proverb remains as relevant today as it was in ancient times, serving as a succinct yet powerful reminder of our fundamental connection to the land and the importance of agriculture in sustaining life. By embracing its lessons of self-reliance, environmental stewardship, and a strong work ethic, we can navigate the challenges of the modern world while building a more resilient and sustainable future for generations to come.

Beyond Fear

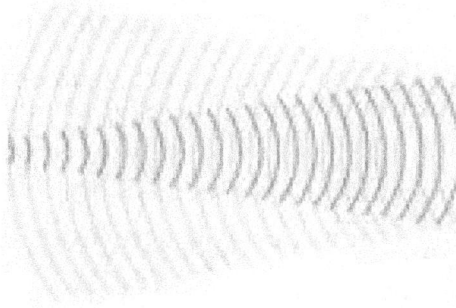

*"After all, it is when a lion is dead
that a goat plays with its tail."*
~Nigerian Proverb

This proverb conveys a profound message about power dynamics, hierarchy, and the consequences of actions. It is a metaphorical expression often used to highlight the importance of recognizing and respecting authority or strength.

Mark Irabor

The imagery of a lion, symbolizing strength and dominance, contrasts with the goat, which is typically perceived as weaker and more submissive. The proverb implies that the goat only dares to play with the lion's tail when the lion is no longer a threat, emphasizing the importance of respecting authority and power dynamics.

The phrase "after all" implies a specific timing or situation in which certain actions or behaviors are acceptable or possible. It suggests that there are appropriate times for asserting oneself or challenging authority and that recklessness or defiance can have consequences. The proverb also carries a warning about the consequences of challenging those in power. It suggests that challenging or disrespecting authority can be dangerous or ill-advised, as symbolized by the potential consequences of provoking a lion.

At a deeper level, the proverb speaks to the natural order of hierarchy and the importance of maintaining stability and respect within a social or hierarchical structure. It implies that there are consequences for disrupting this order or challenging those in positions of authority as well as the potential dangers of abuse of power by those in authority.

In the early 1990s, a small village named Ogba became the setting for a series of abuses of power by the local police chief and his deputies. Operating with impunity, they concocted false accusations against unsuspecting locals, shattering lives and communities in the process. Fabricating evidence of various crimes, they extorted money from their victims and framed innocent citizens for offenses they never committed.

Their reign of terror lasted over a decade as fear gripped the village and trust in law enforcement eroded. Those who dared to speak out against the corruption faced intimidation and retribution from those sworn to protect them. Behind the shield of their uniforms, the local police chief and his deputies wielded unchecked authority, leaving devastation in their wake.

Finally, in 2006 the truth began to emerge, and the local police chief was apprehended on federal charges. Yet, the scars of their misconduct lingered, haunting the lives of those wrongfully accused. It wasn't until 2008 that justice began to be served, as prosecutors dismissed the cases of 300 victims, seeking to right the wrongs inflicted upon the innocent by those who abused their power.

This proverb speaks to the importance of stability and order within society. Maintaining a sense of structure and hierarchy is essential for societal cohesion in today's fast-paced and often chaotic world. Disregarding, undermining authority, or the abuse of power by those in authority can lead to instability and discord, disrupting the social fabric and impeding progress in our society. It highlights the need for humility and understanding of one's place within the larger framework of society. Just as a goat would not dare to play with a lion's tail while the lion is alive and in control, individuals, especially those in authority, must recognize the boundaries of their authority and act accordingly. Respect for authority fosters a sense of order and mutual respect within society, paving the way for constructive dialogue and cooperation.

Overall, the proverb serves as a timeless reminder of the importance of recognizing authority, understanding consequences, and maintaining stability within hierarchical structures. In today's complex and interconnected world, these lessons remain as relevant as ever, guiding us toward a more harmonious and respectful society.

Ancestral Pride

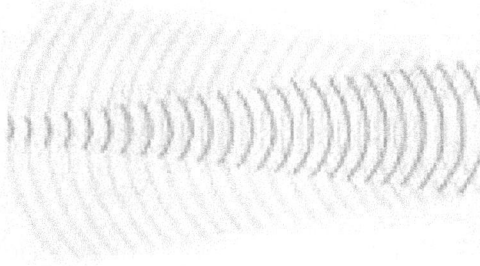

"When a man is proud of his ancestors,
he will always live a worthy life."
~Nigerian Proverb

The statement reflects the profound influence of ancestral pride on an individual's character and actions. This sentiment emphasizes the importance of honoring one's lineage and heritage as a guiding principle for living a meaningful and virtuous life.

Pride in one's ancestors signifies a deep respect for

the traditions, values, and achievements passed down through generations. By acknowledging and honoring the contributions of their ancestors, individuals affirm their connection to a rich cultural heritage and draw inspiration from the resilience and wisdom of those who came before them.

Ancestral pride fosters a strong sense of identity and belonging within individuals, anchoring them to their roots and providing a sense of continuity across time. This connection to one's ancestry serves as a source of strength and resilience, especially during challenging times, as individuals draw upon the lessons and experiences of their forebears to navigate life's obstacles.

Living a "worthy life" encompasses upholding ethical principles, exhibiting moral integrity, and contributing positively to society. Individuals who take pride in their ancestors are more likely to be guided by the values and virtues upheld by their lineage, striving to uphold their family's honor and legacy through their actions and decisions.

Ancestral pride instills a sense of responsibility and accountability in individuals, motivating them to conduct themselves in a manner that reflects positively on their lineage. This sense of duty extends beyond personal achievements to encompass contributions to the greater good of the community heritage for future generations.

The proverb underlines the profound impact of ancestral pride on shaping individual character, values, and behavior. It emphasizes the importance of honoring and preserving one's cultural heritage as a guiding force for leading a purposeful and virtuous life, rooted in respect, identity, and a sense of responsibility to one's ancestors and society as a whole.

In the United States, the flourishing popularity of services like Ancestry.com and 23andMe can be attributed to the widespread desire among individuals to delve into their ancestral origins. These platforms offer a unique opportunity for people to embark on a journey of self-discovery, unraveling the intricate threads of their familial history and uncovering the rich tapestry of their genetic heritage. One such individual who embarked on this quest is my wife, Deborah who seized the chance to explore her ancestral lineage, particularly to ascertain if her forebears hailed from Nigeria.

The allure of tracing one's ancestry resonates deeply within the American cultural landscape, reflecting a broader societal fascination with identity and heritage. In a nation characterized by its diverse mosaic of ethnicities, cultures, and traditions, the quest to unravel the mysteries of one's past holds a profound significance, offering a sense of belonging and connection to a broader historical narrative. For many individuals, including my wife, the prospect of unearthing their ancestral roots represents a deeply personal journey driven by a longing to forge a tangible link to the past and gain insights into their identity.

Against this backdrop, platforms such as Ancestry and 23andMe have emerged as invaluable tools, empowering individuals to embark on a voyage of self-discovery with unprecedented ease and accessibility. Through the analysis of DNA samples and genealogical records, these services provide users with a comprehensive glimpse into their genetic ancestry, unraveling the intricate web of familial connections that span generations and continents. This innovative approach to genealogy has revolutionized the field, democratizing access to ancestral insights and enabling individuals from all walks of life to unravel the mysteries of their past.

My wife's decision to explore her ancestral roots was motivated by a profound curiosity about her familial history and a desire to gain a deeper understanding of her heritage. Like countless others, she was drawn to the promise of uncovering hidden connections and tracing her lineage through the annals of time. In particular, she harbored a keen interest in discovering if her ancestors had originated from Nigeria, a question that had lingered in the recesses of her mind for years.

Echoes of Elders

With the advent of platforms like Ancestry and 23andMe, this quest for ancestral knowledge has been transformed into a tangible reality, allowing individuals like my wife to delve into their genetic heritage with unprecedented precision and depth. Through the analysis of DNA samples, these services provide users with detailed insights into their ancestral origins, tracing the migratory patterns of their forebears and illuminating the diversity of their genetic heritage. For my wife, the process of uncovering her ancestral roots was a deeply transformative experience, imbued with a profound sense of wonder and discovery. As she delved deeper into her familial history, she was captivated by the stories of her ancestors, each one a testament to the resilience and tenacity of the human spirit. She found out that her origins were 22% Cameroon, Congo, and Western Bantu people, 20% Mali, 15% Benin and Togo, 13% Ivory Coast and Ghana, 14% Nigerian and 12% European. With each revelation, she gained a newfound appreciation for the distinct embroidery of her genetic heritage, embracing the rich cultural mosaic that had shaped her identity.

Ultimately, the journey to uncover one's ancestral roots is a deeply personal and transformative experience, offering individuals a profound connection to their past and a greater understanding of their identity. Genetic genealogy and the quest for ancestral knowledge have been democratized, empowering individuals from all walks of life to embark on a journey of self-discovery with unprecedented ease and accessibility. For my wife and countless others, the opportunity to trace their genetic heritage has been a source of profound insight and enlightenment, offering a glimpse into the intricate embroidery of their familial history and a deeper appreciation for the rich diversity of the human experience.

Hunted by Mistake

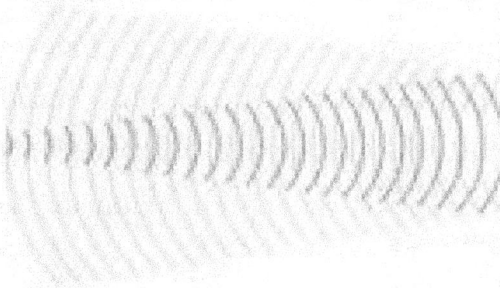

"The day a hunter mistakenly kills a man is the day he is termed a bad hunter."
~Nigerian Proverb

This proverb captures a profound moral lesson about accountability, responsibility, and the consequences of one's actions. This proverb originates from various African cultures and is often used to convey the idea that a single mistake or misdeed can overshadow all previous accomplishments and tarnish one's reputation irreparably.

The primary message of the proverb is the importance of ethical conduct and the consequences of actions. In the context of hunting, it shows the gravity of mistakenly causing harm to a human being, emphasizing the need for us to exercise caution, skill, and responsibility in our pursuits.

The proverb highlights the concept of accountability and the significance of reputation in African societies. Like individuals in any profession, Hunters are judged not only by their skills but also by their integrity and ethical behavior. The act of mistakenly killing a human being is considered a grave error that reflects poorly on the hunter's competence and character.

It also emphasizes the sanctity of human life and the importance of respecting it. It serves as a reminder that human beings should be treated with utmost care and consideration, and any action that results in harm or loss of life, even unintentionally, is unacceptable. While the proverb carries a stern warning about the consequences of mistakes, it also implies the potential for growth and redemption. Like all individuals, hunters are fallible and may make errors, but what ultimately defines them is how they respond to those mistakes. Learning from errors, taking responsibility, and striving to prevent similar incidents in the future are essential aspects of personal and professional development.

For instance, when children gain access to their parents' firearms and unintentionally injure their siblings, the parents may face criticism and legal repercussions for failing to store the firearm securely. This incident underscores the crucial significance of ethical behavior, accountability, and valuing human life. It underscores the imperative for individuals to exercise prudence and responsibility in their conduct, as a single error can cast a shadow over their reputation and lasting legacy. As we live in a world where individuals are constantly under scrutiny and held accountable for their actions, this proverb highlights the need for integrity and moral fortitude. It emphasizes the idea that even a single mistake can tarnish one's reputation and legacy, especially when that individual is held in high esteem or occupies a position of authority.

In today's society, where public figures and leaders are subject to intense scrutiny and criticism, the repercussions of a misstep can be magnified. Whether in politics, business, or any other sphere of influence, individuals are expected to uphold high standards of ethical conduct and face severe consequences when those standards are breached. Moreover, this proverb underscores the inherent value of human life and the responsibility we have to protect it. Equating the accidental loss of life to the failure of a hunter, emphasizes the gravity of such a mistake and the importance of preventing harm to others through our actions.

In our fast-paced digital age, where news travels swiftly and public perception is volatile, the significance of ethical behavior and personal accountability cannot be emphasized enough. This proverb serves as an expressive reminder to uphold integrity and responsibility across every facet of our lives, lest a single error come to overshadow our entire character and legacy.

The Carpenter's Dilemma

"Why does a carpenter not have
chairs in his house?"
~Nigerian Proverb

At its core, this proverb speaks to the paradoxical scenario where someone possessing a particular skill or profession neglects to apply it to their own life. The carpenter, skilled in the art of crafting furniture, including chairs, is depicted as lacking these basic amenities in his dwelling. This apparent contradiction prompts reflection on the reasons behind such oversight.

One interpretation of the proverb revolves around neglect. The carpenter, engrossed in fulfilling external demands and catering to the needs of others, inadvertently overlooks his necessities. This neglect may stem from a sense of duty or obligation to prioritize external responsibilities over personal well-being.

It suggests that the carpenter's focus on other priorities detracts from addressing his needs. Whether driven by financial concerns, societal expectations, or personal aspirations, the carpenter may allocate his time and resources towards endeavors other than furnishing his own home.

The tendency to overlook one's own needs while attending to the needs of others. The carpenter, dedicated to perfecting his craft and serving clients, may neglect the importance of creating a comfortable living environment for himself and his family. It is essential to consider the cultural context in many African societies; communal values and interdependence play a central role in shaping individual behavior. The carpenter's inclination to prioritize the needs of others over his own reflects the communal ethos prevalent in African cultures.

Echoes of Elders

The proverb emphasizes the importance of self-sufficiency and self-care within the context of communal living. While communal support is valued and encouraged, individuals are also expected to attend to their well-being and address their personal needs. Beyond its cultural and metaphorical significance, the proverb "Why does a carpenter not have chairs in his house?" offers practical insights applicable to various aspects of life:

It also serves as a poignant reminder of the importance of self-care and prioritizing one's well-being. Just as the carpenter must carve out time to craft chairs for his home, individuals should allocate resources and attention toward nurturing their physical, emotional, and mental health. Achieving a balance between external obligations and personal needs is essential for holistic well-being. While attending to professional responsibilities and societal expectations, individuals must also cultivate a nurturing environment within their homes.

The proverb encourages individuals to leverage their skills and resources for their benefit. Whether it be carpentry, cooking, or any other talent, individuals should not neglect opportunities to enhance their quality of life through the application of their abilities.

By exploring its interpretations, cultural insights, and

real-life applications, we gain a deeper understanding of the wisdom embedded within this proverbial expression. As we navigate the complexities of contemporary life, the lessons imparted by this proverb remain relevant, guiding us toward a more balanced and fulfilling existence. In essence, the carpenter's lack of chairs in his own house symbolizes the universal tendency to prioritize external demands at the expense of personal needs.

By heeding the message of this proverb, we empower ourselves to create homes that are not only physically comfortable but also nurturing sanctuaries that reflect our values, aspirations, and well-being.

Every day, as I go to work, I pass a young man who flips for change on the corner street on my way to work. He is homeless and appears at times on drugs. I often wonder how he would be if he had the support to get off drugs and have a safe place to live and the tools to get a job.

Applying this proverb to our society, we ignore the extreme increase of homelessness in our cities, our veterans are not getting the best medical treatment that they deserve as the best soldiers in the world, our schools are understaffed, teachers underpaid, and our citizens are ever burdened with medical bills when they are sick or visit the hospitals. Yet, we are providing aid to other countries instead of first taking care of our own.

In the end, the proverb serves as a powerful catalyst for introspection and societal critique. When applied to contemporary society, it unveils a stark reality of neglect towards pressing issues such as homelessness, inadequate healthcare for veterans, underfunded education systems, and burdensome healthcare costs. Realigning societal priorities requires a concerted effort to address systemic inequalities, prioritize human welfare over profit, and uphold moral obligations to the most vulnerable members of society. Only through introspection, advocacy, and collective action can societies bridge the gap between rhetoric and reality, ensuring that every individual's fundamental needs are met and societal resources are allocated equitably for the betterment of all.

Drowning in Indulgence

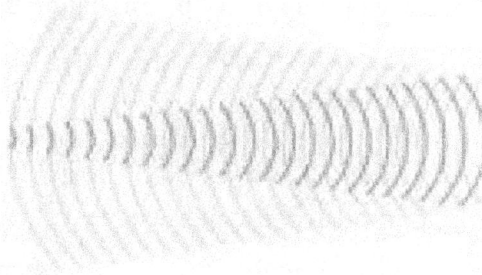

"A man who drinks a lot of palm wine must be ready to drown like a fly in the palm wine keg."
~Nigerian Proverb

In the rich embroidery of Nigerian oral tradition, proverbs stand as pillars of wisdom, capturing profound truths that resonate across generations. Among these timeless gems, this proverb shines a spotlight on the perils of excess and the inevitable consequences. The proverb is not merely a string of words but a poignant reflection on human behavior and the repercussions of unchecked indulgence.

Palm wine, a ubiquitous beverage in many African cultures, serves as the focal point of this proverb. As a traditional alcoholic drink derived from the sap of various palm tree species, palm wine holds a significant place in social gatherings, ceremonies, and everyday life. Its sweet, mildly fermented taste appeals to many and its cultural significance cannot be overstated. However, within the proverb context, palm wine plays a dual role - symbolizing both pleasure and peril.

At its core, the proverb warns against the dangers of excessive consumption, using the imagery of a fly drowning in a palm wine keg to drive home its message. The keg, a vessel of temptation and indulgence, becomes a metaphor for any pursuit or substance that entices individuals into a downward spiral of overindulgence. Just as a fly, intoxicated by the sweet aroma of palm wine, meets its demise in the very source of its pleasure, so too do individuals who succumb to the allure of excess face inevitable downfall.

The comparison between the fly and the individual underlines the universality of human frailty. Like the fly drawn to the palm wine keg, humans are often lured by desires and appetites that promise immediate gratification. Whether it be alcohol, wealth, power, or any other vice, the human tendency to pursue excess can lead to self-destructive consequences. In this sense, the proverb serves as a sobering reminder of the fragility of human nature and the importance of exercising restraint.

Moreover, the proverb carries a moral imperative, emphasizing personal responsibility and accountability. By stating that the man who drinks a lot of palm wine must be "ready to drown," the proverb implies that individuals must confront the repercussions of their actions. In a world where instant gratification often trumps long-term consequences, this message of accountability resonates deeply. It challenges individuals to reflect on their choices and accept the outcomes, whether favorable or adverse.

Beyond its cautionary tale, the proverb also imparts a broader lesson on the virtue of moderation. Embedded within its words is the timeless wisdom that balance is key to a fulfilling life. Just as moderate consumption of palm wine can enhance social gatherings and cultural experiences, moderation in all aspects of life can also lead to greater harmony and well-being. The proverb advocates for a mindful approach to indulgence, urging individuals to temper their desires with prudence and self-restraint.

Furthermore, the proverb's cultural significance extends beyond its moral teachings to reflect the values and norms of

Echoes of Elders

African societies. In many African cultures, communal sharing and moderation are revered virtues that underpin social cohesion and harmony. The proverb's warning against excess aligns with these cultural values, reinforcing the importance of collective well-being over individual gratification. It serves as a reminder that one's actions can have ripple effects within the community and that self-restraint is a personal virtue and a communal responsibility.

In essence, the proverb captures a timeless truth that transcends cultural boundaries. It speaks to the universal human experience of grappling with desires and the consequences of unchecked indulgence. Through its vivid imagery and moral teachings, the proverb imparts a powerful lesson on the virtues of moderation, personal responsibility, and collective well-being.

In a world where excess is often glorified and instant gratification prized above all else, this ancient African proverb stands as a beacon of wisdom, guiding individuals towards a path of balance and mindfulness. Its message resonates across time and space, reminding us of the enduring power of oral tradition to impart timeless truths that illuminate the human condition. As we navigate the complexities of modern life, may we heed the wisdom of our ancestors and tread carefully, lest we, too, find ourselves drowning in the palm wine keg of excess.

When I lived in New Orleans, I knew two guys named

Femi and Balogun. They were a dynamic duo of entrepreneurs whose journey began with promising collaborative efforts in advertising and marketing, propelling their business to unprecedented success. However, as their ambitions soared, their insatiable greed soon clouded their judgment, leading them down a treacherous path of betrayal and downfall.

Femi and Balogun, driven by a shared vision and entrepreneurial spirit, initially joined forces to navigate the competitive landscape of the healthcare industry. Their synergy was palpable, and their business flourished under the banner of mutual respect and collaboration. Together, they harnessed their respective strengths, leveraging innovative marketing strategies and fostering strong relationships within the community.

As their business grew, so did their appetite for success. Fueled by a desire for more significant profits and market dominance, Femi and Balogun's harmonious partnership unraveled. Dissatisfaction seeped into their hearts, overshadowing the achievements they had once celebrated together. Instead of cherishing their joint success, they became consumed by envy and greed, blind to the destructive path they were treading.

The turning point came when Femi and Balogun succumbed to the temptation of cutthroat competition. No longer content with their shared prosperity, they turned on each other with ruthless determination. Poaching employees and customers from one another became fair game as they engaged in a vicious battle for supremacy. What had once been a partnership built on trust and camaraderie devolved into a bitter rivalry fueled by betrayal and deceit.

Amidst the chaos of their escalating feud, Femi and Balogun resorted to spreading malicious rumors and undermining each other's reputations. Their once-thriving businesses became battlegrounds for personal vendettas, with no regard for the collateral damage inflicted on their employees and customers. The toxic environment they created poisoned the well of goodwill they had painstakingly cultivated over the years.

Femi and Balogun's relentless pursuit of more proved to be their undoing. Blind to the consequences of their actions, Femi and Balogun failed to realize that their greed was a double-edged sword, cutting through the very fabric of their success. As their businesses suffered from internal strife and external backlash, they found themselves isolated and weakened, clinging desperately to the fragments of their shattered dreams. In the end, the cost of their betrayal proved too steep to bear. The loss of clientele, once loyal and supportive, marked the final nail in the coffin of their ventures. Femi and Balogun ultimately shut down their formerly successful enterprises due to their insatiable desire for greater wealth and their inability to control their greed.

The tale of Femi and Balogun serves as a cautionary reminder of the perils of unchecked greed and the destructive power of betrayal. What began as a promising partnership fueled by ambition and camaraderie ended in tragedy, leaving behind a legacy of shattered dreams and broken trust. In the unforgiving landscape of the business world, success is fleeting, and true wealth lies not in material gains but in the integrity of one's character.

As the dust settles on their once-thriving enterprises, Femi and Balogun are left to ponder the harsh lessons learned from their downfall. In the quiet solitude of their reflections, they came to realize that true success is measured not by the wealth amassed but by the relationships nurtured and the legacy left behind. Though their journey may have ended in ruin, their story serves as a stark reminder that in the pursuit of greatness, it is integrity and honor that ultimately endure.

A Case of Destiny

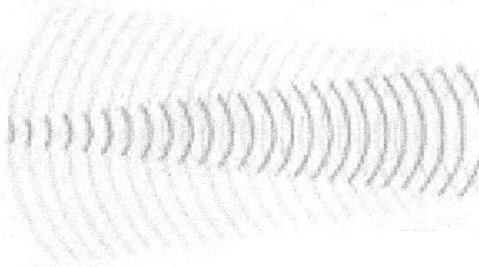

"A man who closes his eyes and enters a grave does not enter the grave which was not meant for him."
~Nigerian Proverb

At the core of the proverb lies the notion of destiny and fate. The metaphor of entering a graveyard with closed eyes symbolizes the journey of life, where individuals navigate through various experiences without complete foresight. Just as one cannot see the graves in a cemetery with closed eyes, individuals cannot predict every twist and turn in their lives.

However, the proverb suggests that regardless of the uncertainties, individuals are guided by a predetermined path, akin to entering the grave that was destined for them. This perspective on destiny aligns with the belief systems of many African cultures, where fate is perceived as predetermined and guided by supernatural forces or spiritual entities. These cultures often interpret events as manifestations of divine will or ancestral influence, emphasizing the interconnectedness between the living and the spiritual realm. Thus, the proverb encourages individuals to acknowledge and accept their predetermined destinies, recognizing human agency's limitations in shaping their lives.

The act of closing one's eyes before entering the graveyard signifies a form of surrender to the unknown and the inevitable. It implies a willingness to embrace whatever fate has in store without resistance or fear. Accepting fate is not passive resignation but rather a profound acknowledgment of the natural order of life and death.

In African philosophical traditions, acceptance of fate is often intertwined with concepts of harmony and balance. Individuals are encouraged to align themselves with the rhythms of nature and the cosmos, understanding that resistance only leads to discord and disharmony. By accepting their predetermined destinies, individuals cultivate a sense of inner peace and tranquility, free from the burdens of anxiety and apprehension about the future. Since certain events in life are beyond human control, just as one cannot choose which grave to enter in the metaphorical graveyard, individuals cannot dictate every aspect of their lives. This recognition of our limitations serves as a humbling reminder of our place within the broader universe of existence.

The proverb encourages individuals to relinquish their illusions of control and surrender to the greater forces at play. Ultimately, it reflects a profound philosophical perspective on life and death that is deeply ingrained in many African cultures. It sums up a holistic worldview that acknowledges the cyclical nature of existence, where life and death are seen as interconnected and inseparable. In this worldview, death is not feared but accepted as an inevitable part of the natural order.

Moreover, the proverb invites contemplation on the transient nature of life and the impermanence of earthly existence. Just as individuals enter and exit the graveyard, so too do they journey through life, leaving behind a legacy that echoes through the annals of time. This philosophical reflection on mortality serves as a poignant reminder of the fleeting nature of human existence and the importance of living purposefully and authentically.

This proverb sums up profound insights into destiny, fate, acceptance, and the human experience. Through its metaphorical imagery, the proverb imparts timeless wisdom about the interconnectedness of life and death and the importance of accepting one's predetermined destiny. It reflects a philosophical perspective on life deeply rooted in many African cultures, inviting individuals to contemplate the mysteries of existence and embrace the inherent uncertainties of the human journey.

This proverb becomes particularly poignant when examined through the lens of two of my friends' experiences during Hurricane Katrina in New Orleans. Despite ignoring evacuation warnings, one friend, Pastor P, survived by being rescued from a rooftop, while another, Yomi, unable to swim, miraculously floated to safety on the body of a drowned victim. These instances serve as powerful examples of how destiny and fate intertwine with human decisions and experiences.

Hurricane Katrina struck New Orleans with devastating force, leaving a trail of destruction in its wake. Amidst the chaos and uncertainty, individuals were faced with life-or-death decisions that would ultimately shape their destinies. My two friends' choices during this critical time would highlight the profound concept of destiny.

Echoes of Elders

Pastor P, despite being urged to evacuate, chose to remain in New Orleans, perhaps underestimating the severity of the impending disaster. However, as fate would have it, he found himself clinging to life on a rooftop as floodwaters engulfed the city. Amid despair, a rescue team arrived just in time to pull him to safety. His survival against the odds serves as a testament to the notion that some forces are beyond human control and that destiny often has its plans.

Conversely, Yomi, also opting to stay behind, found himself in a perilous situation when floodwaters rapidly rose around him. Struggling to stay afloat amidst the chaos, he made a split-second decision to grab onto the body of a drowned victim, using it as a makeshift flotation device. Miraculously, this unconventional act of survival propelled him to safety, underscoring the inexplicable ways in which fate can intervene in the face of adversity.

The experiences of my two friends during Hurricane Katrina also shed light on the importance of acceptance and resilience in the face of adversity. Despite the overwhelming odds stacked against them, both individuals demonstrated remarkable strength and perseverance amid chaos.

For Pastor P, acceptance came in the form of surrendering to the forces of nature and trusting in the possibility of rescue. Despite the harrowing circumstances, he maintained a sense of calm and composure, ultimately placing his fate in the hands of fate.

Similarly, Yomi exemplified resilience in the face of imminent danger. Faced with the prospect of drowning, he refused to succumb to despair, instead seizing upon a fleeting opportunity for survival. His ability to adapt and improvise under duress highlights the indomitable human spirit and its capacity to overcome seemingly insurmountable challenges.

The experiences of my two friends during Hurricane Katrina offer valuable lessons and insights into the complexities of destiny, fate, acceptance, and the human experience. Through their respective journeys, we gain a deeper understanding of the interconnectedness of these concepts and their profound impact on the course of our lives.

These experiences underscore the unpredictable nature of destiny and the inherent uncertainty of the future. Despite our best efforts to control our fate, external forces beyond our control often shape the trajectory of our lives in unexpected ways. It highlights the importance of acceptance in navigating life's challenges. By acknowledging the limits of our control and embracing the inevitability of change, we can cultivate a sense of inner peace and resilience in the face of adversity.

Their experiences serve as a poignant reminder of the resilience of the human spirit. Even in the darkest times, we possess an innate capacity to persevere, adapt, and find hope amidst despair. Through our collective resilience, we can transcend adversity and emerge stronger on the other side.

The proverb resonates deeply with the experiences of Pastor P and Yomi during Hurricane Katrina. Their journeys exemplify the profound interplay between destiny, fate, acceptance, and human experience, offering valuable insights into the complexities of life and the indomitable nature of the human spirit. In the face of adversity, may we draw inspiration from their stories and embrace the unpredictable journey that lies ahead, trusting in the wisdom of destiny to guide us through the storm.

Success in Every Failure

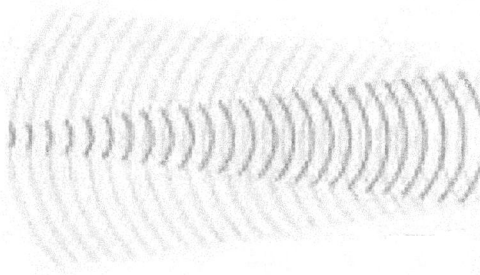

"There are no failures in life but only
a man who knows not to succeed."
~Nigerian Proverb

In life, we encounter a myriad of challenges and setbacks, each presenting an opportunity for growth and learning. Nigerian culture, rich in wisdom and tradition, offers a proverb that captures this profound insight. This proverb not only serves as a beacon of wisdom but also as a guiding principle for navigating life's ups and downs. Through a deeper exploration of this proverb, we uncover its message of resilience, perseverance, and the transformative power of failure.

At first glance, the proverb challenges the conventional notion of failure as an outcome or defeat. Instead, it invites us to reframe our understanding of failure as a temporary setback, a stepping stone to success. In Nigerian culture, failure is not viewed as an endpoint but as a catalyst for growth and self-improvement. By acknowledging that "there are no failures in life," the proverb encourages us to adopt a mindset of resilience, wherein setbacks are seen as opportunities for learning and personal development.

Central to the proverb's message is the notion that failure is not inherent to life but rather a consequence of not understanding how to achieve success. This perspective shifts the focus from external circumstances to internal factors, emphasizing the importance of self-awareness, determination, and perseverance. In Nigerian culture, success is not seen as a stroke of luck or a predetermined outcome but rather as the result of deliberate action and intention. Acknowledging that failure stems from a lack of knowledge or understanding, the proverb empowers individuals to take ownership of their journey and actively pursue success.

Furthermore, the proverb highlights the transformative power of failure in shaping character and fostering personal growth. Setbacks are not viewed as setbacks but as opportunities for self-reflection and improvement. By embracing failure as an integral part of the human experience, individuals can cultivate resilience and adaptability in the face of adversity. The proverb reminds us that our response to failure determines our trajectory in life, highlighting the importance of maintaining a positive mindset and a sense of perseverance.

Moreover, the proverb speaks to the inherent interconnectedness of success and failure in the pursuit of goals and aspirations. Success is often seen as a journey rather than a destination, characterized by twists and turns, ups and downs. Acknowledging that failure is an inevitable part of the journey, the proverb encourages individuals to adopt a growth mindset, wherein setbacks are viewed as opportunities for growth and self-discovery. In doing so, individuals can cultivate resilience and perseverance, enabling them to overcome obstacles and achieve their goals.

The proverb offers a profound insight into the transformative power of failure. By reframing our understanding of failure as a temporary setback and embracing it as an opportunity for learning and growth, we can cultivate resilience, perseverance, and a positive mindset in the face of challenges. This proverb serves as a timeless reminder that success is not defined by the absence of failure but rather by our ability to learn from setbacks and continue moving forward on life's journey.

This proverb explains the notion that failure is not a final destination but rather a temporary setback that can be transformed into a pathway to success through perseverance and learning.

In 1996, when my wife and I decided to go into business, our journey in getting the business started, and operational vividly embodies the essence of this proverb. After we secured the building for our first location, we had difficulty getting an architect and a contractor to help us bring the building to code. Though frustrated by the process, we stood firm and continued our quest. We were able to get the assistance of the architect who helped us over several years in our building process.

After a few years in our first location, we decided to expand our business by building a new facility; that was where the challenge to stand firm and I replayed the proverb in my head over and over as a reminder that "there are no failure in life but only a man who knows not to succeed." To expand our business, we needed a bank loan to build a new structure that would allow us to double the license capacity of our current facility. I went to several banks, but our loan request was denied. I visited twenty-three banks, and our loan request was denied because of the unwritten racial policies of the banks.

In the face of adversity, I encountered rejection from twenty-three different banks. Each denial presented a formidable obstacle, testing my determination and resolve. The tough process of seeking financing for our project was fraught with challenges and stress, yet I refused to be deterred by the setbacks.

The skepticism expressed by an executive from one of the banks, who remarked, "It's not like if you build it, they will come," underlined the doubts and uncertainties that surrounded my endeavor. Despite encountering skepticism and naysayers, I remained steadfast in my belief in the vision I had for the project. Amidst the numerous rejections, I persisted in my pursuit of funding, unwilling to accept defeat. My resilience and perseverance were ultimately rewarded when the twenty-fourth bank approved our loan request. This pivotal moment validated my relentless efforts and served as a testament to the power of perseverance and resilience in overcoming seemingly insurmountable obstacles.

My story serves as a compelling testament to the transformative potential of setbacks. Instead of allowing rejection to define my journey, I chose to view each obstacle as an opportunity for growth and learning. By embracing failure as a catalyst for progress rather than a deterrent, I was able to navigate through adversity and achieve success.

This demonstrates the importance of resilience, perseverance, and unwavering determination in the pursuit of one's goals. One's ability to turn setbacks into opportunities is a powerful reminder of the limitless potential within each of us to overcome challenges and achieve greatness.

Ultimately, obtaining the construction loan for the New Orleans Read Boulevard building exemplifies the profound truth embedded within the proverb, "There are no failures in life but only a man who knows not to succeed." One's unwavering determination, resilience, and willingness to persevere in the face of adversity ultimately will lead to the realization of visions in the pursuit of success.

The Power of
Incremental Increase

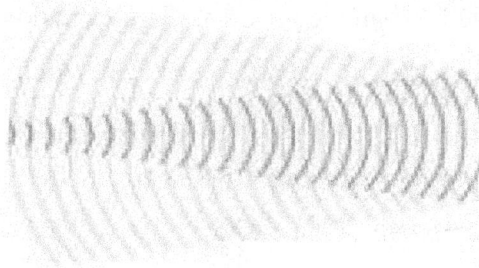

"Little by little, a little becomes a lot."
~Nigerian Proverb

In every culture, proverbs serve as concise expressions of timeless wisdom that express a community's values, beliefs, and experiences. These proverbial expressions often carry profound meanings and serve as guiding principles for individuals navigating life's complexities. This proverb emphasizes the importance of incremental progress and highlights the power of consistent effort in achieving significant outcomes.

This proverb stresses the concept of gradual accumulation leading to substantial results. It speaks to the transformative power of persistence and resilience, suggesting that even the smallest actions, when consistently pursued, can yield remarkable outcomes. This proverb echoes the universal truth that success is often the culmination of sustained effort and perseverance rather than a sudden, monumental achievement.

The metaphorical imagery employed in the proverb is profound yet accessible. By likening progress to the gradual accumulation of small increments, the proverb invites contemplation on the nature of growth and development. It encourages individuals to adopt a patient and methodical approach to pursuing their goals, recognizing that each step, no matter how small, contributes to the larger journey.

In Nigerian culture, proverbs are central to communication, education, and moral instruction. They are passed down through generations, serving as repositories of collective wisdom and cultural heritage. This proverb embodies values which are deeply ingrained in Nigerian society and reflect the importance placed on perseverance, hard work, and community cooperation.

Nigerians are no strangers to adversity, and the proverb serves as a source of inspiration and encouragement in the face of challenges. It reminds individuals that even in the most daunting circumstances, progress is possible through consistent effort and determination. Moreover, the emphasis on incremental growth aligns with the Nigerian ethos of communal solidarity, highlighting the belief that collective action and shared responsibility are essential for achieving meaningful change.

Beyond its cultural significance, the proverb offers practical wisdom for navigating the complexities of daily life. In a world that often glorifies overnight success and instant gratification, the proverb serves as a timely reminder of the value of patience and perseverance. It teaches that incremental progress in learning or skill building can lead to significant expertise over time and consistently saving a small amount of money can accumulate into substantial savings in the long run.

In personal and professional endeavors, the principle of incremental progress can be applied with great effect. Whether pursuing academic goals, building a career, or cultivating relationships, individuals can benefit from adopting a long-term perspective and focusing on consistent, incremental improvement. In Abeokuta, Ogun State, Nigeria, resides Dele, a talented weaver residing in a small village. Dele harbored an ambitious dream of crafting the most exquisite embroidery ever seen in his community. Despite facing discouragement from neighbors regarding his slow pace, Dele persevered diligently, weaving together vibrant threads day after day. His unwavering faith in completing his vision never faltered. Through his unwavering dedication, Dele's masterpiece eventually materialized, serving as a beacon of unity and inspiration within his community. With the completion of his embroidery and with the support of his community, he opened an embroidery school in his community, teaching his craft to young men and women.

The proverb encourages individuals to celebrate small victories along the way, recognizing that each achievement contributes to the larger tapestry of success, no matter how minor. This mindset shift fosters resilience and fortitude, empowering individuals to persevere despite setbacks and obstacles.

In educational settings, this proverb is a powerful teaching tool, imparting valuable lessons about the importance of diligence and dedication. Educators can incorporate the proverb into their curriculum to instill a growth mindset in students, encouraging them to embrace challenges and view failure as an opportunity for learning and growth. Students should be encouraged to spend more time studying on their own and learning a little bit each day and that can eventually result in significant academic success over time. Knowing that consistent effort in studying a subject or learning new skills will gradually build knowledge and expertise in the field of study.

Moreover, this proverb carries a universal inspiration relevant to individuals across diverse ages and backgrounds. Whether one is initiating a fresh endeavor, nurturing a creative pursuit, or advancing on a path of personal growth, the essence of incremental advancement strikes a chord. It stands as a guiding light, instilling the belief that triumph is within reach through persistent dedication and resilience, notwithstanding the challenges faced along the way. Beyond personal aspirations, the wisdom of this proverb extends to financial prudence as well. By diligently setting aside a portion of earnings with each paycheck, one can gradually amass a significant sum over time, ensuring preparedness for future emergencies or long-term goals.

Eventually, this proverb stands as a timeless testament to the power of incremental progress in Nigerian culture and beyond. Its profound message resonates with individuals of all ages, backgrounds, and walks of life, serving as a guiding light in the pursuit of personal and collective goals.

As we navigate the complexities of life's journey, let us heed the wisdom of this proverb, embracing patience, perseverance, and the transformative power of consistent effort. In doing so, we can unlock our full potential and embark on a path towards meaningful and lasting success.

Wisdom's Perspective: The Elder's Insight

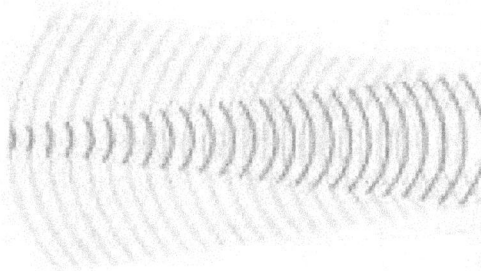

"What an elder can see sitting down,
a young person will not see standing up."
~Nigerian Proverb

The proverb highlights the stark contrast in perspectives between elders and younger individuals. The image of an elder sitting down and a young person standing up symbolizes more than just physical posture; it represents the different vantage points from which each group views the world. The elders, having lived through decades of experience, possess a depth of insight that comes from a lifetime of learning and reflection. In contrast, a young person, with limited life experience, may lack the same level of understanding and awareness.

The proverb suggests that there are certain truths and realities of life that can only be fully grasped from the perspective of an elder. This is not to diminish the experiences or knowledge of younger individuals but to acknowledge the unique wisdom that comes with age and experience. Sitting down implies a sense of contemplation and introspection. These qualities are often cultivated over time and contribute to the elderly's ability to see beyond the surface and discern deeper truths.

Central to the proverb is the concept of intergenerational knowledge transmission, which plays a crucial role in preserving cultural heritage and fostering societal cohesion. Elders serve as custodians of traditional wisdom, passing down their knowledge, values, and customs to younger generations. Through storytelling, mentorship, and everyday interactions, elders impart invaluable lessons that help shape the worldview of younger individuals.

In Nigerian society, respect for elders is deeply ingrained

and serves as a cornerstone of societal norms. The proverb underlines the importance of this respect by highlighting the wisdom that elders possess. By honoring and listening to their elders, younger individuals not only gain access to a wealth of knowledge but also cultivate a deeper appreciation for their cultural heritage.

In Nigerian villages, a longstanding tradition involves resolving disputes through a village council composed of elders. In the early 1990s, in Egoro Amede, Ekpoma, Edo State, Nigeria, a heated disagreement erupted between two families over the property line dividing land inherited from their grandfathers. The younger members of both families staunchly held onto their claims, refusing to consider each other's perspectives. As frustration mounted and the dispute appeared insurmountable, the village council stepped in. Patiently, the elders listened to both sides and then imparted their wise counsel, drawing upon their years of experience and profound understanding of the community's history. Through their guidance, a compromise was reached and agreed upon by the young people involved in bringing peace back to both families.

Life is a multifaceted journey filled with complexities, challenges, and uncertainties. The proverb acknowledges that navigating these complexities requires a nuanced understanding that often comes with age. Elders, having weathered the storms of life, can offer guidance and perspective that can help younger individuals navigate their paths more effectively.

One aspect of life that the proverb alludes to is the importance of patience and perseverance. The image of an elder sitting down suggests a patient and contemplative approach to understanding the world. In contrast, the young person standing up may be more eager to rush forward without fully considering the implications of their actions. Through their experiences, elders have learned the value of patience and the importance of taking the time to carefully observe and analyze before making decisions.

Elders, having lived through various trials and tribulations, possess a resilience that comes from overcoming challenges and setbacks. This resilience is born out of experience and serves as a source of strength and wisdom for both the elderly and younger generations.

At its heart, the proverb underscores the importance of respect for elders within society. In Nigerian culture, as in many other cultures around the world, elders are revered for their wisdom, knowledge, and experience. Respect for elders is not merely a matter of etiquette but a fundamental value that reflects the interconnectedness of generations within the community.

By showing respect for their elders, younger individuals demonstrate an appreciation for the wisdom and guidance that comes with age. This respect fosters a sense of unity and cohesion within the community, strengthening the bonds between generations and preserving cultural heritage for future generations.

This proverb sums up the profound wisdom and insight held by elders. It highlights the importance of intergenerational knowledge transmission, the complexities of life, and the significance of respect for elders within society. Through contemplation and reflection, elders can offer invaluable guidance and perspective that enrich the lives of younger individuals and contribute to the preservation of cultural heritage.

Although my children were born in the United States, I frequently remind them of the traditions I grew up with in Nigeria. I consistently emphasize to them the importance of listening and showing respect to their elders, even when they believe they are correct. I stress that they can learn valuable life lessons from heeding the advice and counsel of their elders.

As we navigate the complexities of life, let us remember the wisdom embedded within this proverb and honor the elders who have paved the way before us.

Recognizing Strength
Within Gentleness

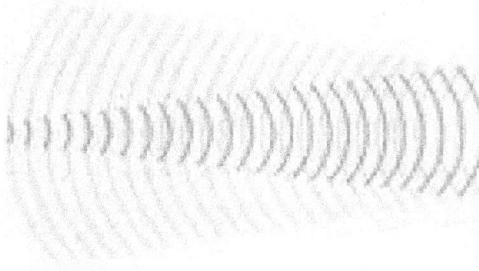

*"Only a fool will take a man's
meekness for weakness."*
~Nigerian Proverb

In our fast-paced and ever-changing world, the interplay between strength and meekness weaves intricate patterns, often misunderstood or overlooked. The proverb serves as a touching reminder of the nuanced nature of human behavior and perception, characterized by dynamic social landscapes and evolving power dynamics. This proverb resonates deeply with us, urging us to reconsider our assumptions and interpretations. Through a lens that integrates cultural wisdom with contemporary realities, the relevance and implications of this proverb can be seen in present-day society.

Meekness, often misconstrued as a sign of weakness, is a trait imbued with profound strength and resilience. In a society where assertiveness and aggression are sometimes glorified as markers of power, the subtlety of meekness is frequently undervalued. However, the proverb expresses that true strength lies not in the ability to dominate or overpower but in the capacity to exercise restraint, empathy, and understanding. The proverb summarizes the essence, challenging the conventional notions of strength and inviting us to delve deeper into the multifaceted nature of human behavior.

One of the most pertinent domains where this proverb's wisdom manifests is interpersonal relationships. In an era dominated by digital communication and fleeting interactions, genuine connection and empathy often take a backseat. The propensity to mistake meekness for weakness can lead to misunderstandings, conflicts, and missed opportunities for meaningful connections. Individuals who display humility and gentleness may be perceived as vulnerable or easily exploitable, yet beneath the surface lies a reservoir of inner strength and resilience.

Echoes of Elders

Still, in the realm of leadership and governance, the proverb assumes heightened significance. Leaders who lead with humility and empathy are sometimes perceived as ineffective or indecisive, especially in environments characterized by cut-throat competition and power struggles. However, history is replete with examples of transformative leaders who wielded their influence with grace and humility, effecting lasting change through their meek yet resolute demeanor.

Moreover, the proverb holds a mirror to societal attitudes towards vulnerability and mental health. In a world that often equates vulnerability with weakness, individuals struggling with mental health challenges or emotional turmoil may find themselves marginalized or stigmatized. The inability to discern between meekness and weakness perpetuates harmful stereotypes and inhibits open conversations about mental well-being. Embracing vulnerability as a sign of strength rather than weakness is essential for fostering a compassionate and inclusive society.

The corporate world, with its emphasis on competition and assertiveness, is another arena where the proverb finds resonance. In environments where success is often equated with aggression and assertiveness, individuals who embody meekness may face challenges in advancing their careers or making their voices heard. However, organizations that value empathy, collaboration, and emotional intelligence recognize the inherent strength in meekness, fostering a culture of inclusivity and innovation.

Besides, the proverb offers insights into the dynamics of power and privilege within society. Those who wield power often exploit the perception of meekness as a weakness to maintain their dominance and control. However, true empowerment lies in recognizing and amplifying the voices of the marginalized and oppressed, acknowledging the strength inherent in their struggles and resilience. The proverb serves as a rallying cry for social justice and equality, challenging systems of oppression and advocating for the empowerment of the disenfranchised.

In the end, the proverb transcends cultural boundaries to offer profound insights into the complexities of human behavior and perception. In a world where strength is often equated with dominance and assertiveness, the proverb reminds us of the inherent strength and resilience beneath the meekness veneer. By challenging our preconceived notions and embracing the sensitivity of human nature, we can foster a more compassionate, inclusive, and empathetic society.

As we navigate the intricacies of interpersonal relationships, leadership, mental health, corporate culture, and social justice, let us heed the wisdom of this proverb and embrace the transformative power of meekness.

Independence Through Practical Experience

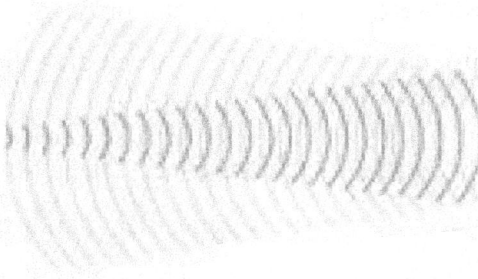

"A lion does not allow its children to live alone until they have once killed an animal in his presence."
~Nigerian Proverb

This Nigerian proverb teaches a profound cultural wisdom that transcends geographical boundaries. It resonates with the universal theme of parental guidance, practical skill acquisition, and the journey toward independence. Through the metaphor of the lion, a symbol of strength and majesty in numerous cultures, the proverb communicates essential lessons about the role of parents in nurturing their offspring and the importance of experiential learning in achieving self-sufficiency.

At its core, this proverb speaks to the fundamental human experience of growth and maturation. Like the lion cubs in the proverb, children rely on their parents for protection, nourishment, and guidance as they navigate the complexities of life. The lion, as a parent, serves as a powerful archetype representing strength, wisdom, and authority.

In many cultures, the lion is revered as the king of the jungle, embodying qualities of leadership and protection. The act of killing an animal in the presence of the lion symbolizes a rite of passage, a crucial milestone that marks the transition from dependence to independence. This act is not merely about survival but also about demonstrating competence and mastery. By requiring their offspring to engage in this activity, the lion parents instill a sense of self-confidence and capability in their young.

Likewise, the presence of the lion during this pivotal moment highlights the importance of mentorship and guidance in the learning process. Just as the lion observes and provides feedback to its cubs during the hunt, parents play a crucial role in imparting knowledge and skills to their children. Through hands-on experience and direct instruction, parents equip their offspring with the tools they need to thrive in the world.

The proverb also emphasizes the value of practical experience in the acquisition of essential skills. In the context of the hunt, the lion cubs must learn to track, stalk, and capture their prey. These skills are not acquired through theoretical knowledge alone but through practice and repetition. Similarly, in human societies, individuals must develop practical skills to navigate the challenges of life effectively.

Moreover, the requirement for the lion cubs to kill an animal before living independently speaks to the concept of earning autonomy through competence. In the natural world, survival depends on one's ability to fend for oneself. By demonstrating their proficiency in hunting, the lion cubs prove that they are capable of meeting their own needs and contributing to their pride.

Beyond its literal interpretation, the proverb carries deeper symbolic meanings that resonate with human experiences. It speaks to the universal journey of growth and self-discovery, where individuals must confront challenges, overcome obstacles, and prove their worth. Just as the lion cubs must face the task of hunting, individuals must engage in various endeavors to develop their skills, build confidence, and assert their independence.

In addition, this proverb highlights the intergenerational

transmission of knowledge and values. Like the lion passing down its hunting skills to its offspring, parents impart their wisdom and traditions to their children, ensuring the continuity of cultural practices and beliefs. This transmission of knowledge strengthens familial bonds and fosters a sense of belonging and identity.

In the present society, the lessons embedded in this proverb remain relevant. As parents, caregivers, and educators, it is essential to recognize the importance of providing opportunities for experiential learning and skill development. By allowing children to engage in hands-on activities and learn through direct experience, we empower them to become competent, self-reliant individuals.

Likewise, the proverb serves as a reminder of the value of mentorship and guidance in the journey toward independence. Just as the lion watches over its cubs during the hunt, adults must offer support, encouragement, and constructive feedback to young people as they navigate the challenges of life. Through mentorship, individuals can learn from the wisdom and experiences of those who have come before them, accelerating their personal and professional growth.

Ultimately, the proverb captures timeless wisdom about the journey toward independence and self-sufficiency. Through the metaphor of the lion and its cubs, the proverb communicates essential lessons about parental guidance, practical skill acquisition, and the importance of experiential learning. By embodying these principles in our own lives and communities, we can empower individuals to thrive and succeed in an ever-changing world.

Overcoming Challenges

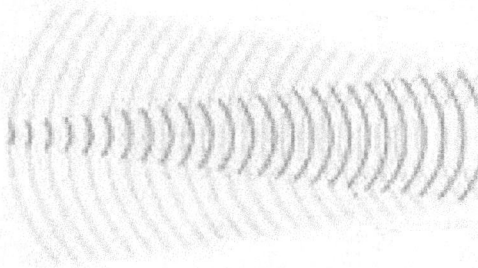

"If a man considers the thickness of the bush,
he will not think of planting yams."
~Nigerian Proverb

The proverb speaks to the importance of focusing on the task at hand rather than getting bogged down by obstacles or challenges. In essence, this proverb encourages individuals to stay focused on their goals and not be deterred by potential difficulties that may arise.

When someone spends too much time worrying about the obstacles that they may face, they are less likely to act and move forward. In the case of planting yams, if a man is constantly preoccupied with the thickness of the bush, he may never actually get around to planting the yams. This can be applied to any aspect of life where one's attention is consumed by potential challenges rather than the desired outcome.

It is easy to become overwhelmed by the potential difficulties that may lie ahead. However, it is important to remember that obstacles are a natural part of any journey towards success. By focusing on the end goal and taking consistent action towards that goal, one can overcome any obstacle that may come their way.

Furthermore, getting stuck in the mindset of focusing solely on obstacles can lead to a defeatist attitude. When one is constantly thinking about the challenges they may face, they are more likely to give up before even trying. Individuals can build resilience and perseverance in the face of adversity by shifting their focus to the end goal and taking positive steps towards that goal.

This proverb serves as a powerful reminder to stay focused on the goal at hand and not be consumed by obstacles.

By keeping one's eye on the prize and taking consistent action towards their desired outcome, individuals can overcome any challenge that comes their way.

Drops of Wisdom

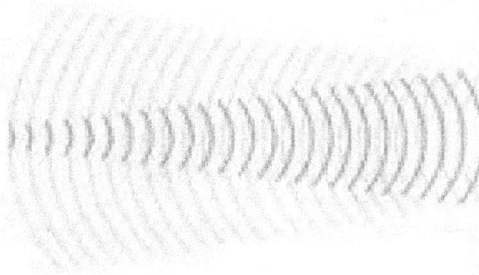

"Once you carry your own water,
you will remember every drop. "
~Nigerian Proverb

This proverb holds a significant meaning in various aspects of life, including self-reliance, perseverance, and gratitude. It reflects the value of personal responsibility and the importance of appreciating the efforts and struggles one goes through to achieve success.

This proverb has its roots in the traditional African culture that emphasizes the importance of self-reliance and hard work. In many African societies, fetching water is considered a daily chore that represents the fundamental necessity of life. This proverb conveys the idea that when one takes responsibility for their own needs and works hard to fulfill them, they will appreciate the value of every effort they make.

In Nigerian history, the struggle for independence and self-governance has been a recurring theme. The Nigerian people have had to fight for their rights, freedom, and dignity in the face of colonialism, corruption, and political unrest. The proverb encapsulates the spirit of resilience, determination, and perseverance that has characterized the Nigerian people throughout history.

Chief Obafemi Awolowo, a prominent Nigerian nationalist and statesman, is one of many figures who advocated for self-reliance, economic empowerment, and education for all Nigerians. His leadership and vision inspired many to work hard and strive for a better future.

The impact of the proverb on Nigerian culture and society cannot be overstated. This proverb serves as a constant reminder of the value of hard work, perseverance, and self-sufficiency. It encourages individuals to take ownership of their lives, responsibilities, and actions, leading to personal growth and empowerment.

In Nigerian communities, the proverb is often used to instill values of diligence, resourcefulness, and gratitude in the younger generation. Parents and elders pass down this wisdom to their children, emphasizing the importance of appreciating the fruits of their labor and never taking anything for granted. This proverb shapes attitudes and behaviors, fostering a culture of self-reliance and resilience in Nigerian society.

Fela Anikulapo Kuti, a legendary Nigerian musician and activist, used his music to convey powerful messages of social justice, resistance, and empowerment. His songs often referenced African proverbs and traditional beliefs, including the importance of self-reliance and self-respect. Fela's influence on Nigerian music and activism has helped popularize and preserve these proverbs' wisdom for future generations.

This proverb can also be interpreted in various ways, depending on the context and individual experiences. Some may view it as a call to self-reliance and personal responsibility, urging one to take charge of their destiny and not rely on others for their needs. Others may see it as a reminder to appreciate the small victories and efforts contributing to larger achievements.

From a cultural perspective, the proverb highlights the communal values of sharing, cooperation, and reciprocity integral to Nigerian society. It emphasizes the interconnectedness of individuals and communities, where everyone has a role to play in supporting each other and working towards common goals. This perspective underscores the importance of unity, solidarity, and mutual assistance in achieving success and prosperity.

Initiatives that encourage youth empowerment, skill development, and entrepreneurship may draw inspiration from the principles reflected in the proverb, fostering a culture of innovation and self-sufficiency among the next generation.

;

Shared Joy,
Solitary Sorrow

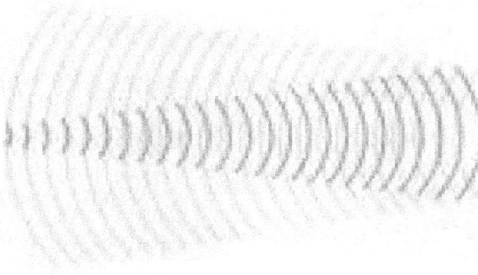

"When a man laughs, the world laughs with him,
but when he cries, he cries alone."
~Nigerian Proverb

The phrase is often attributed to a poem by Sir Thomas More, an English poet and playwriter. It encapsulates that joy is often shared and celebrated collectively, while sorrow is a solitary experience. My Nigerian ancestors also often used this phrase as a proverb. It highlights the importance of empathy and compassion towards those going through difficult times, recognizing that they may be facing their challenges alone.

The idea that joy is shared and sorrow is isolated has been present in various cultures and societies. In many traditional societies, communal celebrations and festivals are common, where people come together to share moments of joy and happiness. These communal gatherings serve as a way for individuals to connect with one another, strengthen social bonds, and experience a sense of belonging and unity. On the other hand, during times of sorrow or distress, individuals may find themselves feeling alone and isolated, as others may not know how to support them or may feel uncomfortable addressing their pain.

The impact of this proverb is significant in shaping how we understand the dynamics of joy and sorrow in our lives. It serves as a reminder of the power of collective joy and the isolation that can accompany moments of sadness. This proverb highlights the importance of being there for others, offering support, and showing empathy towards those who are experiencing difficulties. It encourages us to be more attuned to the needs of others, to reach out and offer a helping hand, and to create a more compassionate and understanding world.

Echoes of Elders

From a positive perspective, the proverb reminds us of the importance of empathy and compassion in our interactions with others. By acknowledging that people may be facing their challenges alone, we are prompted to offer our support and understanding to be a source of comfort and solace during times of need. This can strengthen relationships, foster a sense of community, and create a more caring and supportive society.

On the other hand, there are negative aspects to consider as well. The idea that sorrow is a solitary experience may lead individuals to feel more isolated and alone during difficult times. It can create a barrier to seeking help or reaching out for support, as individuals may fear being judged or not understood. This can exacerbate feelings of sadness and hopelessness, leading to a deeper sense of isolation and despair.

The proverb captures the reality that joy is often shared collectively, while sorrow tends to be a solitary experience. It underscores the importance of empathy and compassion towards those going through difficult times, recognizing that they may be facing their challenges alone. By understanding and embracing this idea, we can strive to create a more compassionate and supportive society where individuals feel heard, understood, and cared for during moments of joy and sadness.

One Step at a Time

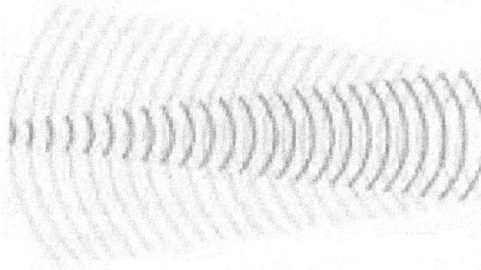

"A journey of 1,000 miles starts with one step."
~Lao Tzu

This phrase is a proverb that dates back to ancient Chinese philosophy attributed to Lao Tzu, the founder of Taoism, emphasizing the importance of taking the first step towards a goal, no matter how daunting it may seem. It suggests that every great journey or achievement begins with a small, simple action and that perseverance and determination are key components in reaching one's destination.

The proverb is a common saying by our elders in Nigeria and expresses the idea that every great achievement begins with a small, deliberate action. This proverb speaks to the importance of taking that first step, no matter how overwhelming the task may seem.

In traditional African societies, proverbs significantly taught important life lessons and values to younger generations. This particular proverb reflects the belief that no matter how daunting a task may seem, progress can be made by taking small, consistent steps forward.

This proverb has taken on added significance in Nigeria with a diverse cultural heritage and a history of resilience in the face of adversity. Nigeria has faced numerous challenges throughout history, including colonialism, political instability, and economic hardship. Despite these obstacles, the Nigerian people have shown remarkable resilience and determination in overcoming adversity. The idea of starting a journey with one step resonates strongly with the Nigerian ethos of perseverance and determination in the face of adversity.

Many individuals throughout history have exemplified the message of the Nigerian proverb, "A journey of 1,000 miles starts with one step." One such figure is Nelson Mandela, the iconic South African leader who fought against apartheid and advocated for peace and reconciliation. Mandela's journey from a political prisoner to the first black president of South Africa serves as a powerful example of how perseverance and determination can lead to profound social change.

The impact of the proverb can be seen in a variety of contexts, from personal growth and self-improvement to societal change and progress. At an individual level, this proverb encourages people to take the first step toward their goals, no matter how small or insignificant they may seem. Individuals can progress toward their objectives and ultimately achieve success by breaking a daunting task into smaller, manageable steps.

The message of this proverb has inspired collective action and social movements that have brought about significant change. For example, the Civil Rights movement in the United States, led by figures such as Martin Luther King Jr., was built on the idea that small, incremental steps toward equality could lead to profound social transformation. By organizing marches, protests, and boycotts, activists raised awareness of racial injustice and pushed for legislative change.

Echoes of Elders

In addition to Nelson Mandela, many other influential individuals have contributed to the field of social change and progress by embodying the message of the Nigerian proverb; one such figure is Mahatma Gandhi, the Indian leader who led a nonviolent resistance movement against British colonial rule. Gandhi's philosophy of nonviolent protest and civil disobedience inspired countless individuals around the world to stand up against injustice and oppression.

Furthermore, Rosa Parks, an African American woman, refused to give up her seat on a segregated bus in Montgomery, Alabama. Parks' act of defiance sparked the Montgomery Bus Boycott and galvanized the civil rights movement in the United States. Her simple yet courageous act of resistance demonstrated the power of taking a stand against injustice, no matter how small the action may seem. This proverb emphasizes the importance of resilience, determination, and perseverance in the face of adversity. Individuals can overcome obstacles and succeed in their endeavors by taking small, deliberate steps toward a goal.

On the other hand, some may view this proverb in a negative light, seeing it as a simplistic or idealistic notion that overlooks the challenges and complexities of achieving long-term goals. Critics may argue that the journey of 1,000 miles is not as straightforward as taking one step and that significant obstacles and setbacks may arise along the way. However, even in the face of adversity, the message of this proverb remains relevant, as it emphasizes the importance of staying committed and focused on the ultimate goal, no matter how difficult the path may be.

As the world faces new challenges and uncertainties, the wisdom of this proverb will serve as a guiding principle for those seeking to make a positive impact in their communities and beyond.

By taking that first step, no matter how small or insignificant it may seem, individuals can set themselves on a path toward growth, transformation, and success. Individuals can overcome obstacles and achieve lasting change by taking small, deliberate steps toward a goal and staying committed to the journey ahead.

As we look to the future, the message of this proverb will continue to inspire and empower us to make a difference in the world, one step at a time..

Wisdom's Currency

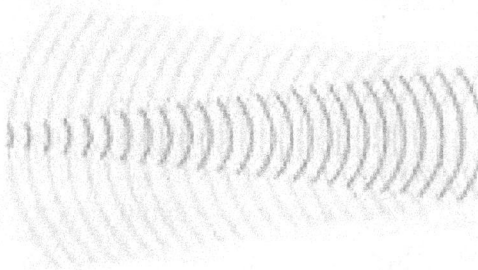

"It's better to be wise than rich and foolish."
~Nigerian Proverb

Throughout Nigerian history, wise leaders, elders, and scholars have played a crucial role in shaping the moral fabric of society and passing down traditional knowledge to younger generations. The proverb has profoundly impacted Nigerian society, influencing people's attitudes, behavior, and beliefs. In a country where materialism and wealth accumulation are often prized, this proverb serves as a reminder of the true value of wisdom and sound judgment. It encourages individuals to prioritize knowledge, learning, and personal growth over superficial gains and shallow pursuit.

By promoting the virtues of wisdom and prudence, this proverb has helped instill a sense of responsibility and accountability in Nigerian society. It urges people to make thoughtful, informed decisions based on reason and good judgment rather than succumbing to greed, impulsiveness, or recklessness. The impact of this proverb can be seen in the way Nigerians approach challenges, solve problems, and navigate complex social situations with grace and composure.

Several influential figures in Nigerian history have contributed to the understanding and dissemination of the proverb. Figures such as traditional rulers, such as the Obas (kings) and Emirs (chiefs), have played a crucial role in preserving and promoting Nigerian proverbs within their communities. These royal leaders serve as custodians of cultural heritage and oral traditions, passing down proverbs and folklore through generations to ensure their continuity and relevance. Their influence extends beyond the confines of their kingdoms, shaping public discourse and social norms based on the values embodied in proverbs like "It's better to be wise than rich and foolish."

By prioritizing wisdom over wealth, individuals can cultivate a deeper sense of self-awareness, ethical integrity, and moral responsibility. Wisdom enables people to navigate life's challenges with grace, resilience, and compassion, fostering harmonious relationships and fostering a sense of community.

Also, wisdom empowers individuals to make informed choices, set meaningful goals, and pursue their aspirations with clarity and purpose. By developing their intellectual faculties and emotional intelligence, people can enhance their well-being, personal satisfaction, and overall quality of life. The pursuit of wisdom not only benefits individuals on a personal level but also contributes to the greater good of society by fostering a culture of learning, innovation, and mutual respect.

Some people may question prioritizing wealth over wisdom in a world driven by economic incentives, social status, and material consumption due to the systemic inequalities, injustices, and power dynamics that can hinder people's ability to access education, pursue intellectual interests, or cultivate wisdom in societies marked by poverty, corruption, and social instability. In such contexts, the pursuit of wisdom may be seen as a luxury reserved for the privileged few, rather than a universal ideal for all.

As Nigerian society grapples with rapid social change, economic uncertainty, poverty, corruption and political challenges, the wisdom embodied in this proverb will serve as a inspiration for people seeking to make a positive difference in their community.

This proverb "It's better to be wise than rich and foolish" calls upon individuals to embrace the transformative power of knowledge, empathy, and wisdom in shaping a more just, equitable, and sustainable future for all. By heeding the lessons of this proverb, we can create a world where wisdom reigns supreme, enriching our lives and inspiring generations to come.

By valuing wisdom over wealth, we can cultivate a deeper understanding of ourselves, our relationships, and our place in the world, guiding our actions with virtue, compassion, and purpose. As we reflect on the profound insights contained in this proverb, let us strive to embody its teachings, embrace its challenges, and realize its transformative potential in our lives and communities.

Wisdom in Love
and Courage

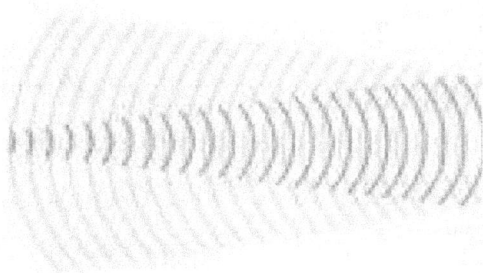

"It is only a brave man that takes the hand of a pretty woman for marriage. But it doesn't mean that the man is brave that he should challenge a lion to a wrestling contest."
~Nigerian Proverb

Nigerian culture boasts a rich embroidery woven with the threads of ancient proverbs, each serving as a vessel carrying wisdom, morals, and life lessons through the ages. Among these venerable sayings, one particular gem gleams brightly: "It is only a brave man that takes the hand of a pretty woman for marriage. But it doesn't mean that the man is brave that he should challenge a lion to a wrestling contest." In the intricate weave of this proverb lies a profound truth – courage encompasses not only daring risks but also the wisdom of discerning choices and the prudence to act accordingly.

These proverbs stand as pillars of Nigerian heritage, steadfastly passed down from generation to generation, their essence infused into the very fabric of society. Within this cultural tapestry, the aforementioned proverb emerges as a beacon, illuminating the significance of courage and resolve in the face of life's myriad choices, especially those concerning matters of love and risk.

In the intricate variety of Nigerian society, marriage occupies a hallowed space, revered as a pivotal milestone demanding valor and unwavering commitment. The act of selecting a life partner is no trivial matter, for it casts a profound shadow upon one's future, shaping the contours of happiness and fulfillment. The image conjured by the proverb – of a courageous man embarking on the journey of matrimony with a beautiful woman – speaks volumes about the essence of authentic love. It whispers of bravery, of determination, and of the unyielding resolve to weather the storms of life hand in hand.

Echoes of Elders

Yet, nestled within the bosom of this seemingly straightforward wisdom lies a nugget of caution, a gentle reminder of the perils that lurk beneath the surface of recklessness. To challenge a lion to a wrestling match, as depicted in the latter part of the proverb, is to court folly of the highest order. It serves as a stark admonition against the hubris of overestimating one's prowess and underestimating the gravity of the situation. Herein lies a testament to the importance of humility and self-awareness, virtues that serve as beacons guiding one through the treacherous waters of temptation and adversity.

The concept of courage, as summarized within the folds of this timeless proverb, has left an indelible mark on the collective psyche of Nigerian society. It has woven itself into the very fabric of attitudes towards relationships, marriage, and the numerous choices that pepper the journey of life. The notion that genuine courage is not merely the audacity to take risks but the sagacity to make prudent decisions and confront challenges with humility has struck a resonant chord with many Nigerians. It has seeped into the marrow of our being, influencing our outlook and shaping our conduct across a multitude of spheres.

In the sacred realm of marriage, the proverb serves as a guiding light, illuminating the path for individuals as they navigate the web of relationships. It stands as a steadfast reminder that true love transcends the superficial veneer of physical attraction, requiring instead a deeper connection rooted in mutual respect, trust, and empathy. By eulogizing the bravery inherent in the act of marrying a beautiful woman, the proverb advocates for the virtues of commitment, fidelity, and perseverance in forging enduring and meaningful relationships.

Thus, the proverb occupies a hallowed place in the complex tapestry of Nigerian culture. It is a testament to the timeless wisdom that courage is not merely the absence of fear but the triumph of wisdom and prudence in the face of adversity. As it resonates through the annals of time, it continues to shape the collective consciousness of a people, guiding them along the path of love, courage, and fulfillment.

The Power of Memory and the Consequences

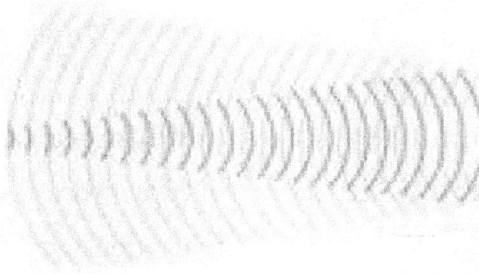

"The axe forgets, but the tree remembers."
~Nigerian Proverb

This proverb is a powerful Nigerian proverb that speaks to the lasting impact of actions and the importance of memory.

It is a poignant reflection of the interconnectedness of actions and consequences, highlighting the resilience of nature and the enduring impact of human behavior rooted in the belief that while individuals may move on from their actions, the repercussions of those actions can persist, shaping the future for themselves and others.

"The axe forgets, but the tree remembers" underscores the importance of accountability, responsibility, and the interconnectedness of all living beings. It serves as a reminder that our actions have far-reaching consequences for us and the world around us. This proverb encourages reflection, introspection, and a deeper understanding of the impact of our choices on others and the environment.

It urges people to consider the long-term effects of their actions and decisions and emphasizes the importance of mindfulness, empathy, and foresight in navigating relationships, conflicts, and challenges. By acknowledging the lasting repercussions of their behavior, individuals can strive to make more informed and ethical choices that contribute to positive outcomes for themselves and their communities.

This proverb also speaks to the consequences of historical injustices, societal inequalities, and environmental degradation. It serves as a call to action for communities to address past wrongs, seek reconciliation and healing, and create a more sustainable and equitable future for all. By recognizing the interconnectedness of humanity and nature, societies can work towards building a more just, harmonious, and resilient world that benefits present and future generations.

The proverb elicits a range of perspectives and interpretations, reflecting the complexity and nuance of human experience. Some may view this proverb as a cautionary tale, warning against the destructive consequences of unchecked power, greed, or negligence. Others may see it as a reminder of nature's resilience and regenerative capacity, which outlasts human transgressions and endures through adversity.

This proverb can be seen as an exploration of memory, trauma, and healing. It prompts individuals to confront past wounds, acknowledge their impact on the present, and work toward reconciliation and restoration. People can cultivate empathy, forgiveness, and growth by recognizing the interplay between memory and action, fostering healthier relationships and communities.

Furthermore, this proverb can serve as a catalyst for social justice, environmental stewardship, and cultural preservation. By recognizing the importance of memory, history, and collective well-being, societies can work towards rectifying past injustices, protecting natural resources, and celebrating cultural heritage. Through dialogue, education, and action, communities can build a more inclusive, sustainable, and harmonious future that honors the wisdom of the past.

Looking ahead, the proverb "The axe forgets, but the tree remembers" is likely to remain a timeless and resonant reminder of the interconnectedness of all life forms and the enduring power of memory. As societies grapple with pressing challenges such as environmental degradation, social inequality, and cultural division, this proverb can guide ethical decision-making, sustainable practices, and inclusive dialogue.

In the digital age, this proverb may take on new forms of expression and dissemination, reaching a global audience through social media, literature, art, and activism. By harnessing the power of technology and storytelling, individuals can amplify the message of this proverb, fostering empathy, solidarity, and positive change on a larger scale. As new generations engage with this ancient wisdom, they can build upon its legacy, reinterpreting it in light of contemporary issues and aspirations.

This proverb encapsulates profound truths about human nature, memory, and interconnectedness. Through its exploration of actions and consequences, history, and resilience, this proverb challenges individuals and societies to reflect on their past, present, and future, striving toward greater understanding, healing, and harmony. By embracing the

Echoes of Elders

wisdom of this proverb, we can cultivate a more compassionate, conscious, and sustainable world for generations to come.

Respecting Others

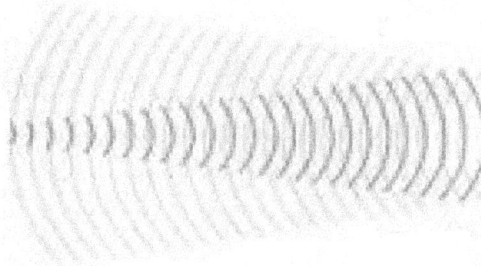

"A man being short does not make him a boy."
~Nigerian Proverb

This proverb emphasizes the idea that physical stature does not determine one's maturity or capabilities. It suggests that qualities such as wisdom, character, and resilience are not contingent upon external appearances, but rather on internal qualities and experiences. This proverb serves as a reminder to judge individuals based on their actions, character, and abilities rather than superficial attributes.

This proverb highlights the importance of looking beyond physical appearances and focusing on the essence of a person. It teaches individuals to respect others regardless of their stature and to value the inner qualities that make someone mature and capable.

Key figures in Nigerian culture have played a significant role in promoting the message of this proverb. Influential leaders, scholars, and cultural icons such as Chinua Achebe have emphasized the importance of seeing people for who they are beyond their physical characteristics. By championing the idea that maturity and capabilities are not determined by height or physical appearance, he has helped shape the societal mindset and promote inclusivity and respect for all individuals.

The impact of this proverb extends beyond Nigerian culture and resonates with people around the world. This proverb serves as a universal reminder to look beyond surface-level characteristics and appreciate individuals for their inner strengths and qualities. In societies that often place emphasis on physical appearance and superficial attributes, this proverb challenges norms and encourages a more holistic and inclusive approach to judging others.

By recognizing that physical stature does not define a person's worth or abilities, individuals are encouraged to cultivate a deeper understanding of one another and embrace diversity. This leads to a more inclusive and compassionate society where people are valued for their character, actions, and contributions rather than their external appearances.

As societies become more globalized and multicultural, the need for understanding and acceptance of others becomes even more critical. This proverb serves as a timeless reminder of the importance of seeing people for who they truly are and appreciating the inherent value and worth that each individual brings to the table.

While the impact of this proverb is largely positive, there are challenges in overcoming prejudices and biases that can hinder its message. Nevertheless, the wisdom of this proverb will continue to inspire people to embrace diversity, cultivate empathy, and appreciate the unique qualities that make each individual valuable.

Nurturing Bonds

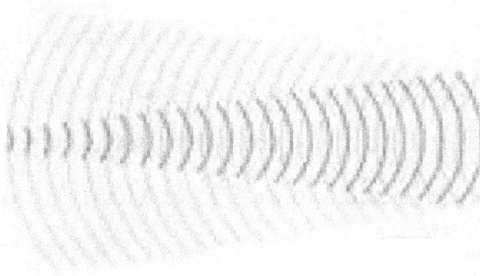

"Always hold a true friend with both of your hands."
~Nigerian Proverb

The proverb is a testament to genuine friendship's value and significance. Rooted in the cultural fabric of Nigeria, this proverb sums up the essence of camaraderie, trust, and reciprocity that defines meaningful relationships. Through its evocative imagery and profound message, the proverb underscores the importance of cherishing and treasuring true friends who offer unwavering loyalty and support.

At its core, the proverb speaks to the intrinsic value of genuine friendship—a bond characterized by mutual trust, loyalty, and emotional support. True friendship is a source of solace, strength, and companionship in a world often marked by superficial connections and transient relationships. The imagery of holding a friend with both hands conveys a sense of reverence and appreciation for the depth of the bond shared between individuals.

Moreover, the proverb emphasizes the reciprocity inherent in genuine friendship. Just as one extends a hand to hold a true friend, so must they reciprocate the same level of commitment, trust, and support. True friendship is not merely a passive presence in one's life but an active and reciprocal exchange of care, understanding, and empathy.

To fully appreciate the depth of the proverb, it is essential to contextualize it within Nigerian culture. Nigeria, a country renowned for its diverse ethnicities, languages, and traditions, holds proverbs in high esteem as repositories of cultural wisdom. Proverbs serve as moral compasses, guiding individuals in navigating life's challenges, ethical dilemmas, and interpersonal relationships.

Echoes of Elders

In Nigerian society, the value of friendship is deeply ingrained, reflecting the communal ethos and interconnectedness that characterize Nigerian culture. Friendships are often regarded as extensions of family, with individuals forming close bonds based on shared experiences, values, and mutual support. The proverb reflects this cultural emphasis on the importance of interpersonal relationships and the nurturing of meaningful connections.

Likewise, the proverb underscores broader cultural values such as loyalty, integrity, and reciprocity. In Nigerian society, loyalty is highly esteemed, with individuals placing great value on the trustworthiness and reliability of their friends and associates. The act of holding a true friend with both hands symbolizes the depth of commitment and loyalty that is expected in genuine friendships.

While rooted in Nigerian tradition, the wisdom encapsulated in the proverb holds relevance in contemporary societies, transcending cultural boundaries and resonating with people across diverse contexts and backgrounds. In an era marked by social isolation, technological disconnect, and interpersonal challenges, the proverb serves as a timely reminder of the importance of cultivating and nurturing genuine friendships.

In the realm of mental health and well-being, the

proverb underscores the therapeutic value of authentic connections and emotional support. Studies have shown that strong social bonds and supportive relationships play a crucial role in promoting resilience, reducing stress, and enhancing overall well-being. By holding true friends with both hands, individuals can create a network of support that sustains them through life's ups and downs.

Furthermore, the proverb holds relevance in the sphere of leadership and community building, it emphasizes the importance of fostering unity, trust, and solidarity. Leaders who prioritize genuine relationships and invest in the well-being of their constituents are better equipped to navigate challenges, inspire collaboration, and promote social cohesion.

Through its evocative imagery and profound message, the proverb encapsulates the essence of trust, loyalty, and reciprocity that define meaningful relationships. As we navigate the complexities of the modern world, may we heed the wisdom of this timeless saying, cherishing and treasuring the true friends who enrich our lives with their unwavering support, understanding, and companionship.

The Weight of Dependence

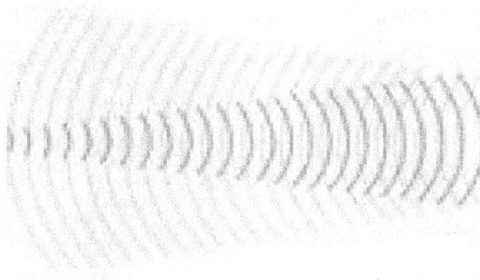

"The one who is carried on one's back cannot back someone else."
~Nigerian Proverb

This proverb conveys the idea that individuals who rely excessively on others for support or sustenance may find themselves unable to extend similar assistance to others. The imagery of being "carried on one's back" suggests a state of dependence or reliance, where one person bears the burden of another. In such a scenario, the individual being carried is preoccupied with their own needs and struggles, leaving little room or capacity to offer aid to others.

This proverb highlights the importance of self-sufficiency and independence, emphasizing the limitations that come with relying heavily on external assistance. It serves as a reminder that true empowerment and resilience stem from one's ability to stand on their own feet and navigate life's challenges autonomously. Furthermore, it underscores the reciprocal nature of support in human relationships, suggesting that those who receive help should aspire to become helpers themselves once they are capable.

However, this support is not seen as an unending obligation but rather as a reciprocal exchange based on mutual respect and empowerment. Individuals are encouraged to strive for self-sufficiency while also recognizing the importance of lending a helping hand to others in need. Thus, the proverb serves as a gentle reminder of the balance between giving and receiving within the social fabric. It prompts introspection about one's reliance on external support and the extent to which it may hinder personal growth and development. Those who constantly depend on others for guidance, resources, or emotional support may inadvertently limit their own capacity for self-reliance and resilience.

Moreover, the proverb underscores the importance of fostering independence and agency in individuals, empowering them to take ownership of their lives and destinies. By cultivating skills, knowledge, and resources, individuals can break free from cycles of dependency and become architects of their own success. This journey towards self-sufficiency benefits the individual and enables them to contribute meaningfully to the well-being of their communities.

At the same time, the proverb serves as a caution against becoming complacent or indifferent to the struggles of others. While striving for self-sufficiency, individuals must remain mindful of the interconnectedness of human experiences and the moral imperative to extend compassion and support to those in need. Thus, the proverb encourages a balanced approach to personal empowerment that encompasses both self-reliance and empathy.

At a societal level, the wisdom encapsulated in the Nigerian proverb holds significant implications for how communities foster resilience, social cohesion, and inclusive development. In contexts marked by economic disparity, social inequality, and systemic barriers, the principle of self-sufficiency takes on added significance as a means of empowering marginalized groups and promoting equitable opportunities.

By promoting policies and initiatives that enable individuals to acquire skills, education, and economic independence, societies can break the cycle of dependency and foster a culture of self-reliance. This requires investments in education, vocational training, entrepreneurship, and social safety nets that equip individuals with the tools they need to thrive independently.

Furthermore, the proverb underscores the importance of building solidarity and collective responsibility within communities. Rather than perpetuating a culture of dependency or paternalism, societies should strive to create supportive environments where individuals are encouraged to help themselves and each other. This entails fostering networks of mutual aid, mentorship, and community empowerment that enable individuals to uplift themselves and their peers.

The proverb reminds us of the importance of cultivating independence and resilience while also recognizing the link of human experiences and the moral necessity to support one another. As societies grapple with complex challenges and disparities, the wisdom embodied in this proverb serves as a guiding light towards inclusive development, social cohesion, and empowerment for all.

Echoes of Endurance

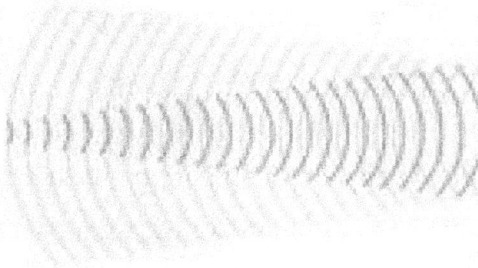

"The buttocks can never be too heavy for the seat."
~Nigerian Proverb

The origins of this proverb can be traced back to traditional Nigerian societies where oral traditions played a crucial role in passing down wisdom and knowledge from one generation to the next. The concept of the buttock being "too heavy for the sit" can be interpreted in various ways, but at its core, it emphasizes the idea that no task or challenge is too difficult to overcome. It signifies the importance of endurance and perseverance in the face of adversity, highlighting the belief that with determination and hard work, one can achieve their goals and fulfill their aspirations.

This proverb has had a profound impact on African societies, influencing the way individuals approach challenges and obstacles in their lives. By emphasizing the value of resilience and perseverance, this proverb has served as a source of inspiration for many, encouraging them to keep pushing forward even in the face of difficulties.

One of the key aspects of this proverb is its ability to instill a sense of hope and optimism in individuals, reminding them that no matter how tough the situation may be, they have the strength and resilience to overcome it. This belief in the power of perseverance has helped many people navigate through tough times, empowering them to continue striving toward their goals and dreams.

Maathai, a Kenyan environmentalist, and political activist who was awarded the Nobel Peace Prize in 2004 for her work in promoting sustainable development, democracy, peace, and dedication to protecting the environment and empowering women in Africa, exemplifies the message of the proverb as she faced numerous obstacles in her quest for social justice and environmental conservation.

While some view the proverb as a call to action, urging people to persevere through challenges and hardships, others see it as a reminder to stay true to one's values and principles, no matter the circumstances. The proverb also serves as a source of motivation and inspiration, empowering individuals to push past their limits and strive for excellence. It encourages people to embrace the challenges they face and use them as opportunities for growth and self-improvement, ultimately leading to personal and professional success.

On the other hand, some may interpret the proverb in a negative light, viewing it as a justification for enduring suffering and hardship without seeking help or relief. This perspective highlights the importance of striking a balance between perseverance and self-care, recognizing that while resilience is a valuable trait, it is equally important to know when to ask for support and seek assistance when needed.

It is evident that the message embodied in the proverb will continue to resonate with individuals across Africa and beyond. In a world that is constantly changing and evolving, the values of resilience, perseverance, and endurance remain timeless and universal, serving as guiding principles for people facing various challenges and obstacles in their lives.

With the rise of globalization and technological advancements, the dissemination of this proverb has been further accelerated, reaching a wider audience and inspiring people from diverse cultural backgrounds. As we navigate through an increasingly complex and uncertain world, the wisdom embedded in this proverb will continue to serve as a source of strength and motivation for individuals seeking to overcome difficulties and achieve their goals.

In summary, this proverb carries profound meaning and significance in African culture, reflecting the values of resilience, perseverance, and determination. Its impact on individuals and societies has been far-reaching, empowering people to face challenges with courage and determination, and inspiring them to strive for excellence in all aspects of their lives.

Beyond Violence

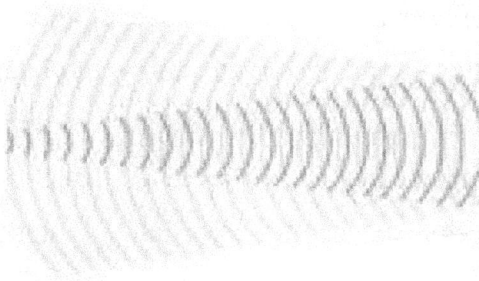

"The day a mosquito lands on your testicles is the day you will know that there are better ways of resolving issues without using violence."
~Nigerian Proverb

The imagery of a mosquito landing on one's testicles, which is a sensitive and vulnerable area for men serves as a metaphor for conflicts and disputes that can arise in life. The experience of feeling discomfort or pain from a mosquito bite can be likened to the negative effects of using violence to resolve conflicts.

Violence is often seen as a quick and easy solution to problems, but it only creates more harm and suffering in the long run. Just as a mosquito bite can cause irritation and discomfort, violence can lead to lasting damage and consequences. By highlighting the idea that there are better ways of resolving issues without resorting to violence, this proverb advocates for peaceful and non-violent approaches to conflict resolution.

To understand the significance of this proverb, it is crucial to delve into the historical context of violence in Africa and the evolution of peaceful conflict resolution methods. Throughout history, African societies have faced various conflicts and challenges, often resorting to violence as a means of dealing with disputes. Wars, ethnic conflicts, and colonialism have all left a lasting impact on the continent, shaping the way in which conflicts are approached.

However, African cultures also have a rich tradition of wisdom and spirituality, which emphasize the importance of peaceful coexistence and harmony. Proverbs, such as the one mentioned, serve as a valuable tool for passing down this wisdom from generation to generation, promoting peaceful solutions to conflicts.

Echoes of Elders

In today's society, where violence is often glorified and used as a means to exert power and control, it is important to remember the wisdom of this proverb. By promoting dialogue, understanding, and empathy, we can find peaceful and constructive ways to address and resolve conflicts. Through communication, compromise, and cooperation, we can build stronger and more harmonious relationships with others.

The impact of this proverb can be seen in various aspects of African society, from grassroots movements promoting peace and reconciliation to government policies that prioritize conflict resolution. By emphasizing the importance of finding alternative ways of resolving disputes, the proverb serves as a guiding principle for individuals and communities seeking to build a more peaceful and harmonious society.

Kofi Annan of Ghana, a diplomat and the seventh Secretary General of the United Nation was one of the figures that dedicated his life to promoting peace, justice, and reconciliation, inspiring others to follow in his footsteps. While the proverb carries a positive message of non-violence and peaceful conflict resolution, it also raises questions about the complexities of dealing with conflict in a globalized world.

As societies continue to grapple with social, political, and economic challenges, finding sustainable solutions to conflicts remains a pressing issue.

Walking the Tightrope

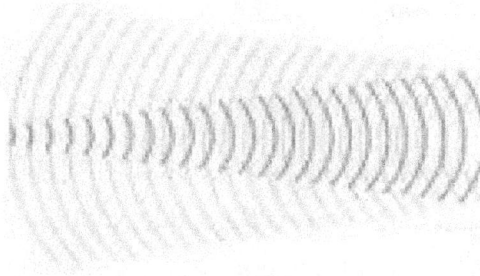

"If you are carrying an egg basket, do not dance."
~Nigerian Proverb

The act of carrying an egg basket is often used as a metaphor for handling delicate or fragile situations with care. Just as one would not want to dance while carrying a basket of fragile eggs, one should exercise caution and restraint in delicate or precarious situations. This proverb serves as a reminder to be mindful of one's actions and to approach sensitive situations with care and consideration, in addition to influencing the way people approach decision-making and interpersonal relationships.

In a society where interpersonal relationships are highly valued, the proverb serves as a reminder to handle delicate situations with care and respect. By encouraging individuals to exercise caution and restraint in their actions, this proverb has helped to foster a culture of mutual understanding and cooperation in Nigerian society.

One positive aspect of the proverb is that it encourages individuals to approach delicate situations with care and consideration. By emphasizing the importance of mindfulness and responsibility, this proverb promotes a sense of awareness and sensitivity in interpersonal relationships.

Another positive aspect of the proverb is its ability to convey complex truths and values in a simple and accessible manner. Proverbs are often used to communicate important lessons and insights concisely and memorable, making them a valuable tool for transmitting cultural knowledge and wisdom.

In African societies, where agriculture and animal husbandry often form the backbone of livelihoods, the imagery of carrying an egg basket holds particular significance. Eggs, fragile and precious, symbolize not only sustenance but also the fruits of labor, patience, and care. The act of dancing, on the other hand, represents frivolity, recklessness, or distraction. Thus, comparing these two elements in the proverb underscores the importance of mindful action and responsible behavior in the face of delicate tasks or situations.

At its core, the proverb speaks to the need for caution and focus when entrusted with tasks of importance or sensitivity. It warns against frivolity or distraction that may jeopardize the successful completion of such tasks. Just as dancing while carrying an egg basket risks dropping and breaking the eggs, engaging in unnecessary risks or distractions while handling delicate matters can lead to undesirable consequences.

Metaphorically, the egg basket represents any duty, responsibility, or endeavor that requires careful handling and attention to detail. This could range from personal relationships and professional commitments to broader societal issues or leadership responsibilities. The message is clear: when tasked with something delicate or precarious, one must approach it with sobriety, mindfulness, and a sense of duty.

Moreover, the proverb highlights the interconnectedness of actions and consequences. Just as a misstep while dancing can result in broken eggs, a lack of focus or responsibility in handling important tasks can have far-reaching repercussions. In this sense, it serves as a reminder of the ripple effect of our actions and the need to consider the broader impact of our choices.

While rooted in African cultural traditions, the wisdom embedded in the proverb "If you carry an egg basket, do not dance" transcends geographical and cultural boundaries, resonating with people across diverse contexts. In an increasingly fast-paced and distracted world, where multitasking and instant gratification often take precedence, its message of mindfulness, responsibility, and focus holds particular relevance.

In the realm of personal development and self-improvement, the proverb encourages individuals to cultivate qualities such as discipline, patience, and mindfulness in their pursuits. Whether pursuing academic goals, career ambitions, or personal relationships, it reminds us to approach our endeavors carefully, avoiding the temptation of being swayed by distractions or shortcuts.

Similarly, in leadership and governance, the proverb serves as a sobering reminder for those in positions of authority or responsibility. Leaders, whether in the political, corporate, or community spheres, are entrusted with the well-being and interests of those they serve. Just as dancing while carrying an egg basket would betray a lack of concern for the eggs' safety, leaders must prioritize the needs of their constituents or stakeholders and act with integrity, foresight, and accountability.

Moreover, the proverb has implications for broader societal issues, such as environmental conservation, social justice, and ethical decision-making. In confronting complex challenges, whether climate change, inequality, or systemic injustice, societies must heed the wisdom of cautious, responsible action. Like custodians of fragile eggs, we are stewards of our planet, our communities, and our shared future, and we must act accordingly.

Lastly, the proverb captures a timeless truth about responsibility, caution, and the importance of focus in navigating life's delicate tasks. Rooted in African cultural traditions yet universally applicable, its message resonates across diverse contexts, offering valuable insights for personal growth, leadership, and societal progress. As we navigate the complexities of the modern world, let us heed the wisdom of this proverb, approaching our endeavors with mindfulness, responsibility, and a sense of duty, lest we risk breaking the fragile eggs entrusted to our care.

Cultivating Calm

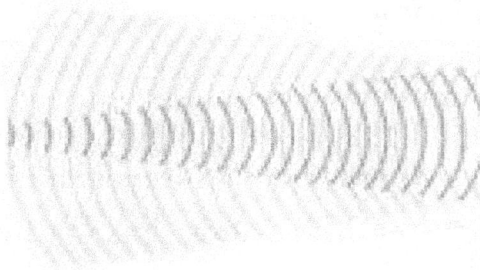

"Master your emotion.
A calm mind will handle any situation."
~African Proverb

This is not a traditional African proverb in the sense that it doesn't have a specific origin tied to African folklore or culture. However, it does reflect a sentiment found in various cultures and philosophical traditions around the world, emphasizing the importance of emotional mastery and maintaining a calm demeanor in the face of challenges. Similar sentiments can be found in many cultures' proverbs and teachings.

"Master your emotion. A calm mind will handle any situation." This is a powerful statement that captures the wisdom of controlling one's emotions and maintaining a sense of calm in the face of adversity. While the origins of this proverb are not definitively African in nature, it resonates deeply with many African cultures and philosophies that value emotional intelligence and inner peace.

The idea of mastering one's emotions and cultivating a calm mind has been a prevalent theme in various cultures and civilizations throughout history. This principle is reflected in the philosophies of many African tribes and societies that prioritize harmony with oneself and the environment.

The impact of this proverb is far-reaching and multifaceted. On an individual level, embracing this mindset can lead to improved emotional regulation, enhanced decision-making skills, and greater overall well-being. By learning to manage their emotions and maintain a sense of calm, individuals can approach difficult situations with clarity and perspective, allowing them to respond thoughtfully rather than impulsively.

Echoes of Elders

In a societal context, the collective adoption of this proverb can foster a culture of emotional intelligence, empathy, and conflict resolution. When individuals prioritize mastering their emotions and cultivating a calm mind, they contribute to a more harmonious and cooperative community where communication is open, understanding is promoted, and unity is strengthened. The proverb invites a range of perspectives and interpretations, each shedding light on different aspects of emotional intelligence and mental resilience. From a psychological standpoint, this proverb underscores the significance of self-awareness, self-regulation, and empathy in promoting mental well-being and interpersonal relationships. By mastering their emotions and cultivating a calm mind, individuals can foster emotional intelligence, adaptability, and psychological resilience, enabling them to navigate life's challenges with grace and fortitude.

From a spiritual perspective, the proverb speaks to the timeless quest for inner peace, transcendence, and enlightenment. By attaining mastery over their emotions and achieving a state of inner calm, individuals can align themselves with the higher truths of existence, tap into their innate wisdom and intuition, and connect with the universal source of life energy. This transcendent state of consciousness opens the door to profound insight, creativity, and spiritual growth, allowing individuals to transcend their egoic limitations and embrace a more expansive and interconnected worldview.

The proverb offers a multitude of positive aspects that can benefit individuals, societies, and the world at large. Individuals can enhance their relational skills, problem-solving abilities, and overall quality of life by cultivating emotional intelligence and mental resilience. A calm mind enables individuals to approach challenges with clarity, creativity, and compassion, fostering a sense of inner peace and well-being that radiates outwards to others.

The collective embrace of this proverb can lead to greater harmony, cooperation, and social cohesion. By promoting emotional mastery and mental fortitude, communities can transcend conflict, division, and discord and cultivate a culture of empathy, understanding, and mutual respect. This emotional intelligence and inner peace foundation provides the necessary framework for resolving conflicts, building consensus, and forging meaningful connections across diverse cultures and perspectives.

Despite its many positive qualities, the proverb also has potential negative aspects that warrant consideration. In some cases, the relentless pursuit of emotional mastery and mental calmness can lead to suppression of genuine emotions, denial of valid concerns, and detachment from the complexities of human experience. This stoic detachment can create a facade of impenetrability and invincibility that isolates individuals from their true feelings, inhibits authentic expression, and hinders genuine connection with others.

Furthermore, the pressure to maintain a constant state of calmness and composure can become a burden for individuals who are struggling with mental health issues, trauma, or overwhelming stress. In a society that values emotional stoicism and mental fortitude, those who are vulnerable or in need of support may feel marginalized or overlooked, perpetuating a culture of silence, stigma, and shame around mental health challenges. The expectation to always "have it together" and stay composed under pressure can exacerbate feelings of inadequacy, self-doubt, and isolation, leading to a further deterioration of mental well-being.

The future development of this proverb lies in its application and adaptation to the evolving landscape of human consciousness, social dynamics, and environmental sustainability. As we confront pressing issues such as climate change, social inequality, and geopolitical conflicts, the imperative to master our emotions and cultivate a calm mind becomes even more urgent. By fostering a culture of emotional intelligence, mental fortitude, and compassionate action, we can forge a more peaceful, equitable, and sustainable future for generations to come.

Lastly, the proverb sums up a profound truth about the power of emotional intelligence and mental resilience in navigating life's challenges with grace and fortitude.

The Tale of Jealousy's Sting

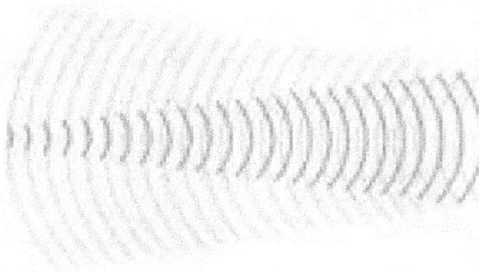

*"If there is no enemy within,
the enemy outside can do us no harm.."*
~African Proverb

In a charming Egoro community of Edo State in Nigeria nestled within rolling hills and lush greenery, there dwelled a young girl named Amara. Amara was known throughout the community for her kindness and generosity. She had a close-knit circle of family and friends who supported her endeavors and cheered her on as she pursued her dreams of going to college in the United States.

One day, as Amara sat on a wooden bench in front of her house, her grandmother approached her with a solemn expression. "My dear Amara," her grandmother began, "I have a tale to share with you, a tale of the delicate balance between trust and betrayal."

Curious, Amara leaned in closer, eager to hear her grandmother's wisdom. "Long ago," her grandmother began, "a young woman named Aisha lived. Aisha was blessed with a loving family and devoted friends who cherished her dearly. But amidst the bonds of friendship and family, jealousy lurked like a shadow, waiting to cast its dark spell."

Amara listened intently as her grandmother recounted the story of Aisha and the perils of envy. "There came a time when Aisha began to make strides in her life, achieving success and recognition in her endeavors," her grandmother continued. "But within her circle of family and friends, jealousy took root in the heart of one who should have been her staunchest supporter."

As the tale unfolded, Amara learned of the insidious nature of jealousy and its destructive power. She listened with a heavy heart as her grandmother described how the green-eyed monster had consumed Aisha's once-trusted friend, turning her against her with envy and resentment.

"Driven by jealousy," her grandmother explained, "the friend sought to sabotage Aisha's happiness and success, spreading rumors and lies to tarnish her reputation. In her blind pursuit of envy, she became the enemy that threatened to tear Aisha down."

Amara shuddered at the thought of such betrayal within the bonds of friendship and family. She realized the truth in her grandmother's words – that sometimes, the greatest threats to our well-being come from those closest to us.

"But fear not, my dear," her grandmother reassured her, placing a comforting hand on her shoulder. "For in every tale of betrayal, there lies a lesson of resilience and strength. Remember the wisdom of the ancient proverb: 'If there is no enemy within, the enemy outside can do us no harm.'"

With those words etched in her heart, Amara pledged to tread with caution in her relationships, mindful of the enemy within that lurked in the shadows of jealousy and envy. She understood that true strength lay not in the absence of adversaries but in the courage to confront and overcome them.

As Amara ventured forth into the world, she carried with her the lessons of her grandmother's tale, weaving the threads of trust and loyalty into the fabric of her relationships.

And though she knew that jealousy's sting could strike unexpectedly, she remained steadfast in her resolve to guard against the enemy within.

Years passed, and Amara grew into a woman of grace and wisdom, guided by the timeless truths passed down through generations. And though the shadows of jealousy may linger on the horizon, she faced each day with courage and resilience, knowing that the strength of her spirit would always prevail.

In the end, the tale of jealousy's sting served as a beacon of light in the darkness, illuminating the path to true understanding and forgiveness. And as Amara looked out upon the world with eyes filled with compassion, she knew that the bonds of family and friendship would forever endure, unbroken by the whispers of envy and resentment.

The wisdom embedded in this proverb has transcended generations and cultures, offering valuable insights into the complexities of human nature and the dynamics of conflict resolution.

It reflects the belief that mentally, emotionally, and spiritually balanced individuals are better equipped and incredibly resilient to handle external challenges and conflicts. The idea of an "enemy within" alludes to the internal struggles, fears, insecurities, and negative beliefs that can sabotage one's well-being and hinder personal growth. By conquering these internal enemies, one can cultivate inner strength, resilience, and self-confidence, which act as powerful shields against external threats and adversities.

In the modern context, this proverb continues to resonate with individuals seeking personal growth, self-realization, and conflict resolution. By acknowledging and addressing their internal conflicts, traumas, and limitations, people can embark on a transformative journey of emotional intelligence, self-awareness, and self-compassion, which are essential ingredients for building healthy relationships, overcoming challenges, and achieving success.

However, it is essential to recognize that the journey of self-improvement and self-discovery is not without its challenges and setbacks. Inner demons such as self-doubt, fear, insecurity, and self-sabotage can often resurface during times of stress, uncertainty, and vulnerability, making it difficult to maintain a sense of inner peace and equilibrium. In such moments, it is crucial to remember that seeking support from mentors, counselors, coaches, or spiritual guides is not a sign of weakness but a strength. They can provide valuable insights, perspectives, and tools for navigating the complexities of the inner world and cultivating a resilient mindset.

This proverb offers a timeless wisdom that transcends cultural, geographical, and historical boundaries. It serves as a reminder of the importance of self-awareness, self-mastery, and self-compassion in navigating the complexities of human relationships, conflicts, and adversities. By embracing the principles of this proverb, individuals can embark on a transformative journey of personal growth, inner healing, and a profound understanding of themselves and others.

Pillars of Strength

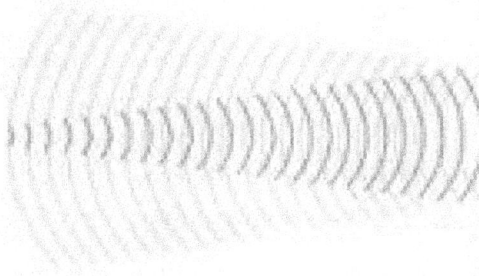

*"Leaning against the pillar of a house
does not make one the owner."*
~Nigerian Proverb

Nigeria, a land rich with culture and wisdom, has a special

proverb: "Leaning against the pillar of a house does not make one the owner." It might sound simple at first, but let me tell you, it's packed with meaning!

In the center of the village stands a big, sturdy pillar holding up the roof of the chief's house. This pillar is strong and dependable, just like the wise elder of the village.

In the village, a young man named Kofa was known for being very lazy. He spent most of his days lounging under the shade of the big tree, avoiding any work. One day, as Kofa was taking his usual afternoon nap, he heard a loud crash. Startled, he looked around and saw that the pillar of his family's house had collapsed! Everyone in the village rushed to help, trying to hold up the heavy roof with their hands.

But as hard as they tried, the roof kept sinking lower and lower. That's when they realized something important: Kofa, the lazy young man, had been leaning against the pillar for so long that it weakened and finally collapsed.

In Nigerian culture, the pillar of a house represents strength, support, and stability. Just like the pillar holds up the roof of a house, there are people in our lives who support us when we need it most—our parents, teachers, and elders. But when someone leans too heavily on others without doing their fair share of work, it's like weakening the pillar of a house. Eventually, it might give way, causing problems for everyone around.

Two friends, Tunde and Emeka, lived in the same village

as Kofa. They were both hardworking boys who helped their families with chores and always lent a hand to their neighbors.

A big storm hit the village one day, and many houses were damaged. Tunde and Emeka didn't hesitate to jump into action. They went from house to house, offering help to repair roofs, clear debris, and support their fellow villagers in any way they could.

Their efforts didn't go unnoticed. The senior elder of the village praised them for their hard work and dedication, calling them the pillars of the community.

Tunde and Emeka were like pillars in their village. They didn't just stand by and watch when trouble struck—they stepped up and offered their support, just like the strong pillar of a house.

Being a pillar means being dependable, trustworthy, and willing to help others in need. It means working hard, not just for yourself, but for the betterment of your community.

Remember the Nigerian proverb, "Leaning against the pillar of a house does not make one the owner." It teaches us the importance of being reliable and supportive, just like the strong pillar that holds up a house.

Don't be like Kofa, leaning on others without doing your part. Instead, strive to be like Tunde and Emeka, pillars of strength in your community, ready to lend a hand and make a positive difference in the lives of those around you.

Beyond Bananas

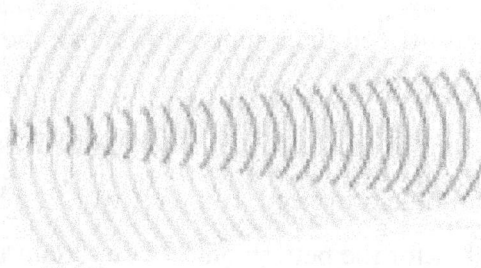

*"You cannot convince a monkey that
honey is sweeter than a banana."*
~African Proverb

This is a popular saying that is often attributed to African
culture. It reflects the innate nature and preferences of
individuals, suggesting that some people are unwilling to

change their beliefs or opinions, no matter how compelling the argument or evidence may be.

The use of animals in African proverbs is a common trope, as it allows for complex ideas to be conveyed in a simple and easily understandable manner. Monkeys, in particular, are often used to represent stubbornness, ignorance, or a lack of comprehension. In this case, the monkey's preference for bananas over honey symbolizes a person's preference for the familiar and comfortable, even if there may be something better available.

Honey and bananas are both sweet, but they represent different choices and possibilities. Honey may be more rare, valuable, or luxurious than bananas, but the monkey's attachment to what it knows and is familiar with prevents it from recognizing or appreciating the potential benefits of trying something new. This can be seen as a metaphor for human behavior, where people may resist change or reject new ideas, even if they are objectively better or more advantageous.

The proverb can also be interpreted as a reminder of the importance of open-mindedness, curiosity, and willingness to consider different perspectives. It suggests that rigid adherence to one's existing beliefs or preferences can limit one's ability to grow, learn, and explore new opportunities. By being willing to try new things, challenge assumptions, and question their own biases, individuals can expand their horizons, discover new possibilities, and ultimately improve their quality of life.

In conclusion, "You cannot convince a monkey that honey is sweeter than a banana" is a thought-provoking proverb that highlights the limitations of stubbornness and close-mindedness.

It encourages people to be open to new ideas, experiences, and perspectives, and to be willing to challenge their own beliefs in order to grow and evolve. While its origins may be uncertain, its message resonates across cultures and time, serving as a timeless reminder of the importance of curiosity, flexibility, and openness to change.

The Pursuit of Inner Peace

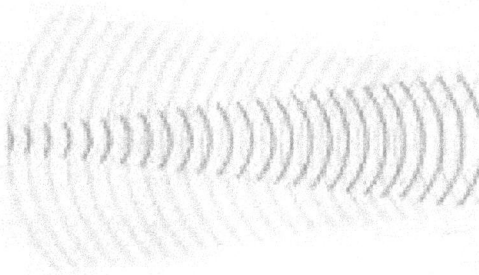

"Don't count what you have lost.
See what you have left."
~African Proverb

This particular proverb encourages individuals to focus on what they still possess rather than dwelling on what they have lost.

In life, it is inevitable that we will encounter losses and setbacks. Whether it be the loss of a loved one, a job, a relationship, or a material possession, it is easy to feel overwhelmed by the sense of emptiness and grief that comes with it. However, this proverb reminds us to shift our perspective and look at the positives that still exist in our lives. Instead of wallowing in self-pity and despair, we are encouraged to take stock of what we still have - whether it be the love and support of family and friends, our health, skills, or opportunities for growth and new experiences.

On August 23, 2005, a big storm started forming in the Bahamas. The next day, it turned into a tropical storm. A weather expert named Bob Breck warned people in New Orleans that the storm could be very dangerous if it went into the Gulf of Mexico. He said, "Leave the city if the storm goes into the Gulf!" The storm quickly moved into the Gulf and got stronger.

On August 29, 2005, Hurricane Katrina hit south Louisiana, but it shifted a bit to the east, so New Orleans didn't get hit directly. However, the storm caused a lot of damage to New Orleans and nearby areas in Mississippi and Alabama. The flood barriers in New Orleans broke, and more than 1800 people died. There was also a lot of property damage, including our house and three preschools we owned.

About ten days after the hurricane hit, my wife and I went to see how bad the damage was. It was really awful. Our house and preschools were wrecked, and I couldn't help but cry. I realized it would be hard for us to go back and live in New Orleans.

Echoes of Elders

We went back to Houston and talked about what to do next. We decided it would be better for our family to stay in Houston. The schools and the environment there were better for our kids, even though moving was tough.

Despite the challenges, we decided to rebuild. We focused on what we still had instead of what we lost in Hurricane Katrina. We felt lucky to have our family safe and together. That was what mattered most to us.

By focusing on what we have left, we are able to see the potential for rebuilding and moving forward. We are reminded that despite the losses we may have experienced, there are still blessings and opportunities to be grateful for. This mindset of gratitude and resilience can help us to navigate through life's challenges with a sense of hope and optimism.

Moreover, the proverb also serves as a reminder of the impermanence of life. Losses are a natural part of the human experience, but they do not define us. Instead of being consumed by grief and regret, we are encouraged to embrace the present moment and make the most of what we have. By adopting a mindset of abundance rather than scarcity, we can cultivate a sense of contentment and fulfillment that transcends our material possessions.

This proverb teaches us to focus on the positives in our lives, even during loss and adversity. By embracing what we have left with gratitude and resilience, we can find strength and joy in the face of life's challenges. In the end, it is our perspective and mindset that shape our experiences and determine our ability to thrive in the face of adversity. So, let us heed the wisdom of this proverb and strive to see the abundance that still surrounds us, even in moments of loss.

Recognizing Your
Potential

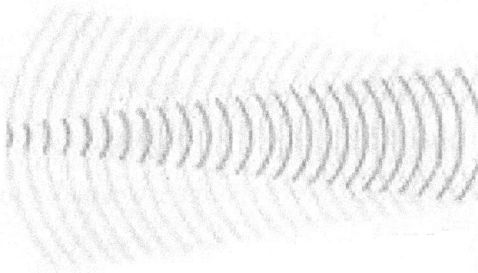

"A bird that knows the use of its feathers
does not fly close to the ground."
~African Proverb

At first glance, this proverb may seem straightforward - after all, birds use their feathers for flight, so of course, they wouldn't fly close to the ground. However, beneath the surface lies a deeper meaning that speaks to the idea of understanding one's own potential and not settling for mediocrity.

In literal terms, a bird that flies close to the ground risks injury or danger. By utilizing its feathers, it can soar to greater heights and reach its full potential. Likewise, as human beings, understanding our own skills, talents, and strengths allows us to excel and succeed in life. By harnessing our abilities and talents, we can achieve great things and avoid falling into the trap of underestimating ourselves.

Imagine a bird soaring high in the sky, its feathers shining in the sunlight as it gracefully glides through the air. This bird is confident in its abilities and knows how to use its feathers to its advantage. It knows that flying close to the ground is risky and limits its potential.

Just like this bird, we too have special talents and skills that can help us reach new heights. When we understand and use these talents effectively, we can achieve great things and avoid unnecessary risks.

There was a young boy named Jamil who attended one of our after-school program facilities in New Orleans who loved to paint. He had a natural talent for art and could create beautiful masterpieces with just a few strokes of his brush. Despite his talent, Jamil was often shy and unsure of himself. He would often second-guess his abilities and doubt if he could ever become a successful artist.

One day, Jamil's art teacher noticed his talent and encouraged him to enter a local art competition. Jamil hesitated at first, fearing that he would not be good enough to compete against other talented artists. But his teacher assured him that he had a gift and just needed to believe in himself

With his teacher's encouragement, Jamil decided to enter the competition. He worked hard on his painting, pouring his heart and soul into every brushstroke. When the day of the competition arrived, Jamil's painting stood out among the rest. The judges were amazed by his talent and awarded him first place.

Jamil's confidence soared as he realized the power of his talent. He understood that he had a gift for painting and could achieve great things if he believed in himself. Just like the bird that knows the use of its feathers, Jamil soared high in the sky, knowing that he could achieve anything he set his mind to.

Understand and embrace your talents and skills and use them to soar to new heights. Believe in yourself and never underestimate the power of your abilities. Just like the bird in the sky, you have the potential to achieve amazing things when you know how to use your feathers.

By recognizing our abilities, having faith in ourselves, and cultivating self-awareness, we can soar to new heights and achieve our dreams. This proverb serves as a reminder to embrace our potential and not settle for anything less than greatness.

Making Peace

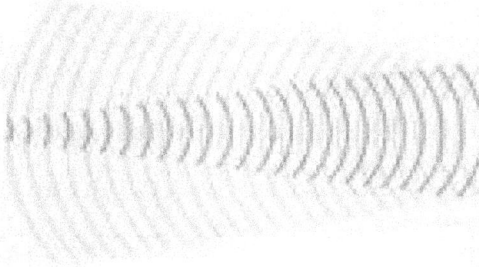

"It is one's enemy that makes death hurtful."
~Nigerian Proverb

Olu and Banjo were good friends and did everything together, from playing soccer to helping each other with their chores. However, one day, a misunderstanding led to a heated argument between them.

Olu felt betrayed by Banjo, and they stopped talking to each other. The rift between them grew wider and wider, until they were no longer on speaking terms. The whole village could feel the tension between the two boys.

Then, tragedy struck. A dangerous illness swept through the village, claiming the lives of many. Olu fell sick and was bedridden, struggling to fight off the sickness. Banjo, although angry with his friend, could not bear to see him suffer.

Banjo put aside his anger and visited Olu every day, bringing him food and medicine. He stayed by his side, offering words of encouragement and comfort. Despite their past differences, Banjo did everything he could to help his friend get better.

Sadly, Olu's condition worsened, and he passed away. The whole village mourned his loss, but it was Banjo who felt the pain the most. He realized that despite their quarrel, Olu was not just a friend but also someone who had made his life better. The regret of not making amends with his friend before it was too late haunted Banjo.

While death is a natural part of life, it is often the relationships we have with the deceased that greatly influence how we experience this loss. When someone we consider an adversary dies, it can evoke a mix of complex emotions such as guilt, regret, anger, and even relief. This can make the grieving process more challenging as we wrestle with these conflicting feelings.

The notion that it is the enemy who makes death hurtful implies that the impact of death goes beyond the mere absence of the person. It highlights the importance of our social connections and how they shape our experiences and emotions. The dynamics of our relationships and the unresolved conflicts we may have with others can profoundly affect our ability to cope with loss.

In the end, Banjo understood the Nigerian proverb, "It is one's enemy that makes death hurtful." He realized that holding onto grudges and harboring hate only causes more pain and regret in the end. It is better to forgive and make peace with those who have wronged us, as life is too short to let animosity ruin relationships.

In Nigerian culture, as well as many African cultures, death is viewed as a communal experience that necessitates collective mourning and support. Losing someone, even if they were perceived as an enemy, can still bring about feelings of sorrow and remorse. This idea reinforces the interconnectedness of humanity and the importance of forgiveness and reconciliation, even in death.

And so, Banjo learned the importance of forgiveness and reconciliation, and vowed to never let anger come between him and his loved ones again. The village saw the boys' story as a lesson in the power of forgiveness and understanding, and they lived harmoniously ever after.

The proverb serves as a reminder of the intricacies of human relationships and the profound impact they have on our emotional well-being in times of loss. Grief can be a complicated and painful process, but finding peace and healing often requires acknowledging and addressing our feelings toward those we may have perceived as adversaries

Staying Humble

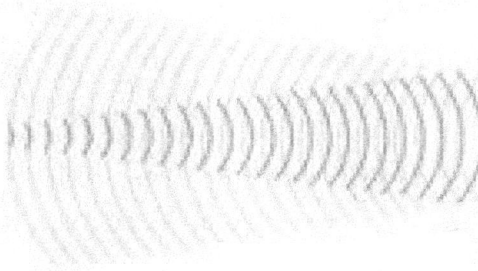

"You don't start licking salt simply because you are wealthy."
~Nigerian Proverb

In life, it is important to remain grounded and humble regardless of one's wealth or status. This sentiment is beautifully captured in this proverb.

The underlying message of this proverb is one of caution against arrogance and frivolous behavior. Salt is a common household item that is used to enhance the flavor of food. However, licking salt is not a common practice and is often associated with cravings or indulgence. By suggesting that one should not start licking salt simply because they are wealthy, the proverb is advising individuals not to engage in unnecessary or excessive behaviors just because they have the means to do so.

Wealth can bring about a sense of entitlement and privilege, but it is important to remember that true success is not measured by material possessions alone. It is easy to lose sight of what is truly important when surrounded by luxury and abundance. The proverb serves as a reminder to stay true to oneself and to not let wealth change one's values and principles.

In a society that values material wealth and extravagance, it can be tempting to flaunt one's riches and indulge in extravagant luxuries. However, this proverb warns against such behavior and encourages individuals to remain humble and grounded. It emphasizes the importance of staying true to one's roots and not allowing wealth to cloud one's judgment.

In due course, the message of this proverb is universal and can resonate with people from all walks of life. It serves as a timeless reminder to stay humble, grounded, and true to oneself, regardless of one's wealth or status. It is a valuable lesson that can guide individuals on their path to success and fulfillment, reminding them that true happiness and contentment come from within, not from material possessions.

The Dreamer's Authority

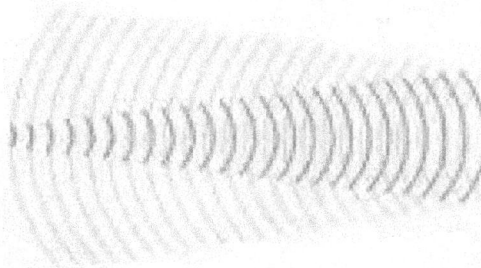

"You don't argue about a dream with its dreamer."
~Nigerian Proverb

This proverb highlights the importance of respecting a person's dreams and aspirations, regardless of how unrealistic or far-fetched they may seem to others.

Echoes of Elders

In Nigerian culture, dreams are often seen as a window into the subconscious mind, revealing hidden desires, fears, and aspirations. Dreams are believed to have symbolic meanings and hold significant spiritual and mystical value. As such, it is considered rude and disrespectful to dismiss or argue about someone's dreams, as doing so can be seen as challenging the dreamer's personal beliefs and experiences.

The idea that one should not argue about a dream with its dreamer reflects the principle of empathy and understanding that is deeply ingrained in African culture. It emphasizes the importance of listening and respecting others' perspectives, even if they may seem illogical or irrational to us. By acknowledging and validating someone's dreams, we show our support and encouragement for their personal growth and development.

Likewise, this proverb can also be interpreted as a reminder of the power of imagination and creativity in shaping our reality. Just as dreams can inspire and motivate us to pursue our goals and aspirations, engaging with the dreams of others can open our minds to new possibilities and perspectives. By embracing the dreams of others, we can cultivate a culture of collaboration and mutual understanding that benefits both individuals and communities.

The proverb embodies the timeless wisdom and values that are cherished in Nigerian and African cultures. It serves as a reminder to approach others with respect, empathy, and an open mind, and to appreciate the power of dreams in shaping our beliefs and aspirations. Through this mindset, we can foster a culture of understanding and unity that celebrates the diversity of human experiences and perspectives.

Fortifying Foundations

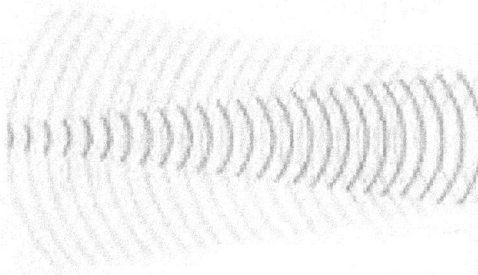

"He who builds a house with leaves,
should expect the storm."
~Nigerian Proverb

This proverb holds deep meaning and significance, serving as a valuable lesson for individuals seeking to make sound decisions and choices in their lives.

The essence of this proverb lies in the concept of being prepared for challenges and obstacles that may come in one's life. It warns against taking shortcuts or making hasty decisions that may lead to negative consequences in the future. Building a house with leaves symbolizes creating something flimsy and temporary, lacking the strength and stability to withstand the harsh conditions of a storm.

In practical terms, this proverb emphasizes the importance of careful planning, diligence, and foresight in any endeavor. It serves as a reminder that taking the easy way out or cutting corners may result in disaster or failure down the line. Just as a house built with leaves cannot withstand a storm, so too will a poorly planned or hastily executed project inevitably crumble under pressure.

Furthermore, this proverb also underscores the value of investing time, effort, and resources into creating a solid foundation for success. It highlights the importance of patience, perseverance, and commitment to achieving long-term goals and aspirations. By taking the time to build something of lasting value and quality, individuals can better prepare themselves for any challenges or adversities that may come their way.

Overall, this Nigerian proverb serves as a timeless piece of wisdom that speaks to the universal truth of the importance of resilience, foresight, and careful planning in all aspects of life. It serves as a poignant reminder to always strive for excellence, to never settle for mediocrity, and to always be prepared for the storms that may come our way.

The Tale of the Dancer

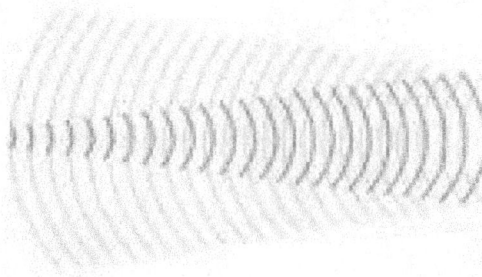

"If someone says he or she is a good dancer, don't argue with them; call a drummer."
~African Proverb

The proverb conveys the idea that one should rely on the expertise of others to judge a certain skill or ability rather than simply taking someone's word for it. In this case, calling a drummer implies seeking the opinion of someone with a deeper understanding of music and rhythm, which can be applied to various aspects of life beyond dance.

Once upon a time, in a small village in Africa, there lived a young girl named Nia. Nia loved to dance and would often boast about her dancing skills to anyone who would listen. She would twirl and stomp her feet, believing she was the best dancer in the village. However, not everyone was convinced of her talent.

One day, a wise elder in the village overheard Nia bragging about her dancing abilities. He chuckled to himself and decided to teach her a valuable lesson. The elder approached Nia and said, "If someone says he or she is a good dancer, don't argue with them; call a drummer."

Confused, Nia asked the elder what he meant by that. The elder explained that in African culture, dance and music are intertwined. While a good dancer can move gracefully and fluidly, the drummer sets the rhythm and brings the dance to life. Without a skilled drummer, even the best dancer would struggle to keep time and stay in sync with the music.

Intrigued by the elder's words, Nia decided to put his advice to the test. She called upon the village's best drummer, a young boy named Kwame, and asked him to play while she danced. As soon as Kwame started drumming, Nia felt a surge of energy and excitement. She moved in harmony with the beat, her body responding to the rhythm as if it were second nature.

Nia's realization was profound – a good dancer shines brightest when accompanied by a talented drummer. She expressed her gratitude to Kwame for his music and promised to always seek out the help of a drummer before showcasing her dance moves in the future.

Drumming, a central element in African music traditions, is not just about creating rhythms and beats. It carries rich cultural meanings, symbolizing different aspects of life, and is a powerful tool for communication and community bonding. In many African societies, drummers are not just musicians but highly respected individuals who possess a deep knowledge of music and are able to convey complex messages through their drumming, making them the perfect authority to judge a dancer's skill.

The impact of the proverb lies in its emphasis on humility and seeking advice from those with expertise. It encourages individuals to recognize the importance of experience and skill in evaluating one's abilities and fosters a sense of respect for different forms of knowledge. By highlighting the role of the drummer as a knowledgeable authority on music and rhythm, this saying promotes the value of collaboration and learning from others in order to improve oneself.

Some may see the proverb as a call for humility and self-awareness, reminding individuals to seek feedback and guidance from those with greater expertise. Others may view it as a caution against arrogance and overconfidence, urging people to acknowledge the limits of their own knowledge and skills.

The proverb carries valuable lessons about humility, respect for expertise, and the importance of seeking advice from others. In a world where self-promotion and ego often take center stage, the wisdom of calling a drummer for guidance serves as a reminder to remain grounded and open to learning from those who have mastered their craft.

The moral of the story is that collaboration and teamwork are essential to achieving greatness. No matter how skilled we may be in our talents, there is always room for improvement and growth when working with others. Just like Nia needed Kwame's drumming to elevate her dancing, we can all benefit from the support and expertise of those around us.

By recognizing the contributions of others and working together towards a common goal, we can achieve extraordinary results beyond what we could accomplish alone. So next time you feel proud of your abilities, remember to call a drummer – because true greatness is found in teamwork and collaboration.

The Unfaithful Wife's Rhythm

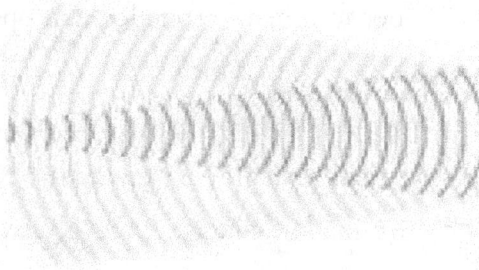

"An unfaithful wife is like a big drum. One person carrying it while another is playing it."
~African Proverb

This proverb delves into the complex themes of betrayal and deceit within relationships, painting a vivid picture of one person bearing the weight of infidelity. At the same time, another is complicit in causing harm.

The cultural significance of this proverb is deeply rooted in traditional African societies, where marriage was revered, and infidelity was a deeply felt betrayal. In many African cultures, women were expected to uphold fidelity and loyalty, and any deviation from this was met with severe repercussions.

The drum, a ubiquitous musical instrument in African cultures, symbolizes the heartbeat of the community and is often used in ceremonies and rituals. By likening an unfaithful wife to a big drum, the proverb vividly illustrates how infidelity disrupts the harmony and rhythm of the community, much like a drum being played out of tune.

On the other hand, the proverb also raises questions about the roles and responsibilities of both parties in a relationship. While the unfaithful wife is likened to a big drum, burdened by the weight of her actions, the person playing the drum is complicit in causing harm and discord. This dynamic speaks to shared responsibility in relationships and the importance of mutual respect and trust. By unpacking the layers of meaning within this proverb, we can gain insight into the complexities of human emotions and behavior.

In a nutshell, this proverb encapsulates the themes of betrayal, infidelity, and the consequences of deceit within relationships. By examining both the positive and negative aspects of this proverb, we can better understand the complexities of human relationships and the importance of loyalty and trust. As we look to the future, we must reflect on this proverb's lessons and strive to cultivate healthy and respectful relationships based on mutual understanding and compassion.

Civility

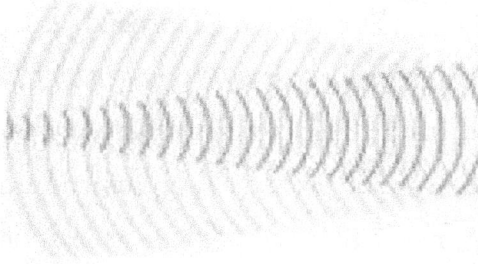

*"A woman is not a banana to be
shared or given as a present."*
~Nigerian Proverb

The proverb speaks to the importance of respecting women as individuals rather than treating them as objects to be exchanged or controlled. This proverb highlights the need to recognize women's autonomy and agency in making their own choices, especially in matters of marriage and relationships.

The concept of women's rights and gender equality has been a longstanding issue in many societies around the world, including Nigeria. Traditionally, women were often considered property or objects to be bartered in exchange for goods, land, or status. They were expected to fulfill certain roles and duties within the household and community, with their voices and opinions often marginalized or ignored.

In Nigeria, as in many other cultures, marriage was often arranged by families for economic or social reasons rather than based on love or mutual consent. Women had little say in whom they married, and their wishes and desires were often discounted in favor of patriarchal norms and traditions. This lack of autonomy and agency led to generations of women being treated as commodities rather than as equal partners in relationships.

The impact of this proverb, is profound and far-reaching. The proverb challenges traditional notions of women's roles and rights in society by asserting that women are not property to be exchanged or controlled. It serves as a powerful reminder of the need to respect women's autonomy and agency, particularly in the context of marriage and relationships.

The proverb also highlights the importance of valuing

women as individuals with their own thoughts, feelings, and desires. It calls attention to the harmful consequences of treating women as objects or possessions rather than as equal partners in relationships. By emphasizing the importance of consent and choice in matters of marriage, the proverb encourages a shift towards more equitable and respectful attitudes towards women.

There are various perspectives on the proverb reflecting the diverse attitudes and beliefs surrounding women's rights and gender equality. Some may view the proverb as a powerful statement of women's autonomy and agency, advocating for the recognition of women as individuals with the right to make their own choices and decisions.

Others may interpret the proverb as a critique of traditional gender roles and expectations, highlighting the need to challenge patriarchal norms that devalue women and limit their freedoms. The proverb can also be seen as a call to action to promote gender equality and empower women to assert their rights and assert their voices in society.

In analyzing, it is important to consider the broader social, cultural, and historical context in which it is situated. The proverb reflects deep-seated beliefs and attitudes towards women and their roles in society, as well as the power dynamics that shape gender relations.

This proverb challenges normative ideas about women's worth and value by challenging the notion that women can be treated as commodities or possessions. It asserts the importance of recognizing and respecting women's autonomy and agency, particularly in matters of marriage and relationships. The proverb can be seen as a rallying cry for gender equality and women's empowerment, urging society to acknowledge and affirm women's rights and dignity.

This proverb is a powerful reminder of the need to recognize and respect women as individuals with rights and agency. The proverb challenges traditional notions of women's roles and rights in society by asserting that women are not objects to be exchanged or controlled. It calls attention to the harmful consequences of treating women as commodities or possessions and advocates for the promotion of gender equality and women's empowerment.

As society continues to grapple with issues of gender inequality and women's rights, the wisdom of this Nigerian proverb remains as relevant and resonant as ever. By embracing the message of this proverb, we can work towards creating a more just, equitable, and inclusive world for women everywhere.

A Case of Bad Luck

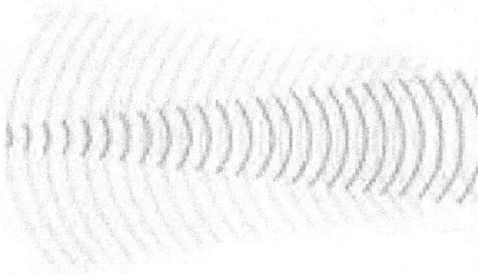

"When bad luck catches you, even a rotten banana can break your teeth."
~Nigerian Proverb

This proverb speaks to the harsh realities of life and the unpredictable nature of fate. It highlights the idea that even the seemingly innocuous can have disastrous consequences when circumstances turn against you. This proverb has deep roots in

Nigerian culture and reflects the resilience and resourcefulness of its people in the face of adversity.

The proverb captures the essence of these struggles, reminding individuals of the importance of vigilance and preparedness in the face of adversity. It serves as a cautionary tale, urging people to be mindful of the potential dangers lurking in even the most mundane situations.

A young man named Ayo once lived in Alayin village in Oyo State, Nigeria. Ayo was known throughout the village for his bad luck. It seemed that no matter what he did, misfortune always followed him like a shadow.

One day, Ayo was walking down the street when he slipped on a banana peel and fell flat on his face. The villagers laughed and shook their heads at his misfortune. Ayo got up, dusted himself off, and muttered to himself a popular Nigerian proverb, "When bad luck catches you, even a rotten banana can break your teeth."

Despite his many setbacks, Ayo remained determined to turn his luck around. He decided to seek the advice of the village elder, who was known for his wisdom and guidance. The elder listened to Ayo's tale of woe and nodded sagely. "You must change your perspective, young man," the elder said. "Bad luck is like a test from the gods. It is up to you to learn from your misfortunes and grow stronger because of them." Ayo took the elder's words to heart and set out to make a change.

He started by volunteering at the local orphanage, helping others in need and spreading kindness wherever he went. Slowly but surely, Ayo's luck began to change. One day, as Ayo was walking down the street, he saw a young boy running towards him with tears streaming down his face. The boy had fallen and scraped his knee badly. Ayo knelt down, comforted the boy, and bandaged his wound. The boy's tears turned to smiles, and he hugged Ayo tightly.

From that day on, Ayo's bad luck seemed to disappear. He found a job at the local marketplace, made friends with the villagers, and even met a kind-hearted woman who stole his heart. Ayo realized that it wasn't bad luck that had been holding him back all this time, but his own negative outlook on life.

As the years passed, Ayo became a respected member of the village, known for his kindness and generosity. Whenever someone in the village faced a challenge, they would say, "Remember Ayo's story – when bad luck catches you, even a rotten banana can break your teeth. But with a positive attitude and a kind heart, you can turn your misfortunes into blessings." And so, Ayo's tale became a legend in the village, a reminder that no matter how bad things may seem, there is always hope for a brighter tomorrow.

The impact of the proverb is profound in its implications

for personal growth and development. It serves as a reminder that life is unpredictable and that challenges can arise when least expected. By acknowledging the fragility of life and the inevitability of setbacks, individuals can better prepare themselves for adversity and cultivate a mindset of resilience.

From various perspectives, the proverb can be viewed as both a cautionary warning and a source of empowerment. On one hand, it reminds individuals of the fragility of life and the need to be mindful of unforeseen dangers. It underscores the resilience and resourcefulness that can emerge in the face of adversity, inspiring people to rise above their circumstances and persevere in the face of challenges.

By embracing the lessons of the past and drawing inspiration from the resilience of their ancestors, people can find strength in the face of adversity and persevere in the pursuit of their goals. The proverb encapsulates the struggles and triumphs of the human experience. It serves as a reminder of the unpredictability of life and the importance of resilience in the face of adversity.

Wisdom Over Wealth

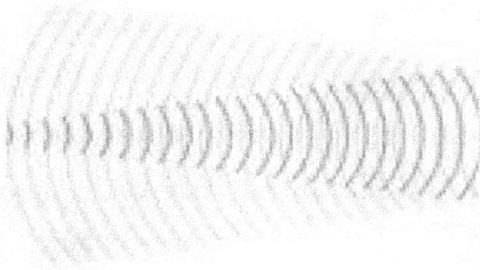

"A man who drives his father's car is not entitled to speak in the council of men who own bicycles."
~Nigerian Proverb

This proverb carries a deep and thought-provoking message about humility, privilege, and personal worth. At first glance, it may seem to simply refer to material possessions and social status. However, upon closer examination, it reveals a complex interplay of societal values, cultural norms, and individual identity.

In many traditional societies, elders and those with wisdom and experience hold a revered position in the community. Younger individuals are expected to listen and learn from their elders before speaking or asserting their opinions. This proverb reflects the idea that privilege and material wealth do not automatically confer wisdom or the right to lead or speak on important matters. Instead, it emphasizes the importance of earning respect through one's actions, character, and integrity.

Figures such as corrupt politicians or wealthy individuals who flaunt their material possessions without regard for others reinforce the negative implications of the proverb. These individuals may prioritize their own interests and personal gain over the well-being of society as a whole. By contrast, those who own bicycles in the proverb symbolize hard work, perseverance, and humility. They earn their place in the council of men through their dedication and commitment, rather than through inherited wealth or privilege.

The proverb continues to resonate in a world marked by inequality, social injustice, and political corruption. It serves as a reminder that true leadership and wisdom are not defined by material possessions or social status, but by one's actions, character, and moral integrity. As societies grapple with issues of wealth inequality, political polarization, and social unrest, the values encapsulated in this proverb remain as relevant as ever.

In conclusion, the proverb offers a powerful message about humility, respect, and personal worth. It challenges individuals to consider the true source of their authority and leadership, and to remember that material possessions do not define a person's worth or value.

Parental Wisdom

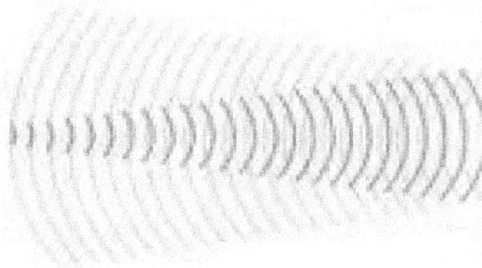

"The child who is not embraced by the village
will burn it down to feel its warmth."
~African Proverb

The proverb speaks volumes about the importance of community and belonging in a child's life. In African culture, the village represents a close-knit community where everyone looks out for each other, offering support, guidance, and love to all its members, especially the young ones.

When a child feels disconnected or alienated from their community, they may resort to destructive behavior in order to seek attention, affection, and a sense of belonging. This proverb emphasizes the idea that when a child's emotional needs are not met within their community, they may act out in an attempt to fill the void, even if it means causing harm to those around them.

Children who grow up without a sense of belonging and without a support system are more likely to struggle with issues such as low self-esteem, depression, anxiety, and even behavioral problems. They may feel unloved, unwanted, and misunderstood. Without the warmth and security of a loving community, they may seek comfort in destructive behaviors or relationships.

Children are inherently social beings who thrive on human connection and relationships. When they feel isolated or abandoned, they may develop feelings of worthlessness, anger, and resentment towards their community. This can lead them to seek validation and acceptance through negative means, such as rebellion, delinquency, or even violence.

The idea of a child burning down the village to feel its warmth is a metaphor for the extreme measures that one might take to seek connection and validation. When a child feels rejected or alienated by their community, they may resort to drastic actions in an attempt to fill the void in their lives. The village, or community, plays a crucial role in shaping a child's sense of identity, self-worth, and belonging. When a child is embraced, supported, and valued by their community, they are more likely to grow up feeling secure, confident, and connected to their roots. On the other hand, when a child is neglected, rejected, or marginalized, they may struggle to find their place in the world, leading to feelings of emptiness, loneliness, and despair.

As adults, it is our responsibility to create a safe, nurturing, and inclusive environment for all children. We must show them that they are valued, respected, and loved. We must offer them guidance, support, and encouragement as they navigate the challenges of growing up. By embracing the children in our village, we can help them to thrive and reach their full potential.

In today's fast-paced, technology-driven world, it is easy for children to feel disconnected and isolated. The rise of social media and the decline of face-to-face interaction have made it more challenging for young people to form genuine connections with others. As a result, many children are struggling with feelings of loneliness and isolation. As members of society, we have a collective responsibility to nurture and protect our children, providing them with the love, care, and support they need to thrive and flourish. By embracing and empowering our youth, we can create a safe and nurturing environment where every child feels valued, appreciated, and included.

In conclusion, the proverb serves as a powerful reminder of the importance of community, connection, and compassion in a child's life. It highlights the profound impact that love, acceptance, and support can have on a child's well-being and development. As we strive to build stronger, more resilient communities, let us remember to embrace and uplift our children, ensuring that they feel loved, welcomed, and cherished every step of the way.

The Snake

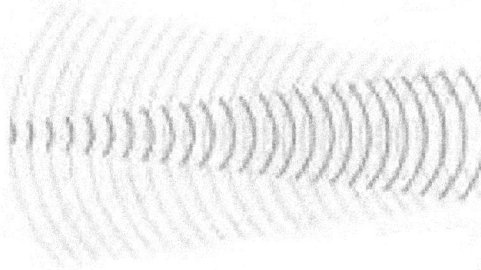

"Beware of green snakes, for success attracts envy."
~Nigerian Proverb

This proverb captures a profound insight into human nature, particularly the dynamics of success and envy within societies. At its core, this proverb warns individuals to be cautious and mindful of the potential consequences that come with achieving success, as it often incites jealousy and resentment from others.

The "green snakes" represent envy, a potent and sometimes hidden emotion that can be likened to a lurking danger. Envy, like a snake, is often camouflaged and strikes unexpectedly, causing harm and disruption. The color green is significant here, symbolizing both envy and the natural world, where snakes are often associated with danger and deceit. Thus, the phrase "green snakes" vividly portrays the insidious nature of envy and the need to remain vigilant against its manifestations.

For "success attracts envy," underscores the reality that achievement and prosperity can provoke envy in others. When individuals achieve success—whether in their careers, relationships, or personal endeavors—they may inadvertently become targets of envy from those who covet their accomplishments. Success, in this context, becomes a double-edged sword, bringing both rewards and risks.

This proverb is deeply rooted in African culture, where communal values and social cohesion are highly valued. In many African societies, the concept of "ubuntu" prevails, emphasizing interconnectedness and collective well-being. Within this framework, individual success is often viewed as a reflection of the community's success, and envy is seen as a threat to the harmony of the group.

Therefore, the warning to "beware of green snakes" serves as a reminder to individuals to tread carefully and consider the broader implications of their achievements on the community. When some individuals perceive others as more successful or fortunate, they may experience feelings of inadequacy or inferiority, fueling their envy.

Moreover, envy often arises in competitive social contexts, where individuals compare themselves to others and strive for status or recognition. Success, as a visible marker of achievement, can trigger envy by highlighting disparities in wealth, power, or prestige. Furthermore, envy is not only directed towards material possessions or external accomplishments but can also encompass personal qualities such as talent, charisma, or popularity. In essence, envy reflects a desire to possess what others have, whether tangible or intangible. This aspect of human nature is universal and transcends cultural boundaries, manifesting in various forms across different societies.

The consequences of unchecked envy can be detrimental, both for the envious individual and the target of their resentment. Envy often breeds hostility, gossip, and sabotage, leading to interpersonal conflict and social tension. In extreme cases, envy can escalate into destructive behaviors, such as aggression, vandalism, or even violence. Moreover, the psychological toll of envy can be significant, eroding trust, damaging relationships, and undermining individual well-being.

In light of these challenges, the proverb offers valuable insights into navigating the complexities of success and envy. First, it encourages individuals to cultivate humility and gratitude for their accomplishments, recognizing the role of luck, effort, and external support in their success. By acknowledging their blessings and remaining grounded, individuals can mitigate the risk of triggering envy in others. Second, the proverb highlights the importance of empathy and compassion towards those who may experience envy.

Rather than dismissing or retaliating against envious individuals, it suggests extending understanding and support, recognizing their struggles and insecurities. By fostering empathy and fostering a sense of solidarity, individuals can promote harmony and cooperation within their communities.

Moreover, the proverb underscores the need for resilience and fortitude in the face of envy and adversity. When confronted with jealousy or criticism, individuals should remain steadfast in their values and aspirations, refusing to be deterred by negativity or setbacks. By maintaining a sense of purpose and determination, individuals can overcome obstacles and continue to pursue their goals with integrity and perseverance.

This proverb offers practical guidance for navigating social dynamics and managing relationships in diverse settings. Whether in the workplace, social circles, or family gatherings, individuals can apply the wisdom of the proverb to navigate potential sources of envy and promote harmony and cooperation. By fostering a culture of mutual respect, appreciation, and support, individuals can mitigate the risks of envy and cultivate positive and fulfilling relationships.

The proverb encapsulates timeless wisdom about the complexities of human nature and the challenges of achieving success in a competitive world. By acknowledging the dangers of envy and adopting strategies to mitigate its impact, individuals can navigate the journey of success with humility, empathy, and resilience. Ultimately, the proverb serves as a reminder to tread carefully, remain vigilant, and cultivate positive relationships based on mutual respect and understanding.

Navigating Love
and Reality

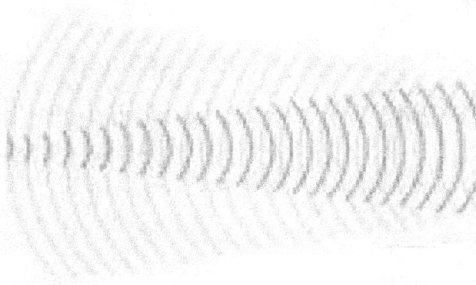

*"Don't be so in love that you cannot
tell when it's raining.."*
~Nigerian Proverb

This proverb captures the idea of caution, advising individuals
not to become so consumed by their emotions that they lose

sight of reality and fail to recognize potential risks or dangers. It encapsulates a profound truth about the delicate balance between the euphoria of love and the necessity of maintaining a clear-eyed view of reality and emphasizes the importance of balance and mindfulness in relationships. Love and romance hold great significance in Nigerian culture and serves as a reminder to individuals to maintain a sense of perspective and not let their emotions blind them to reality.

At its core, the proverb serves as a poignant reminder of the importance of maintaining perspective and awareness, even in the throes of love's fervor. To be "so in love" suggests a state of emotional immersion, where one's perceptions may be colored by the intensity of their feelings. In contrast, the metaphorical "rain" symbolizes the challenges, hardships, and realities of life that may be overlooked or ignored in the haze of infatuation. It cautions against allowing love to cloud our judgment or obscure our understanding of reality. It highlights the need for emotional maturity and discernment, even in the face of overwhelming affection. While love can be a transformative force, it should not blind us to the complexities of the world around us.

The impact of this proverb is profound, shaping the way people approach relationships and navigate the complexities of love and emotion. By cautioning against becoming too immersed in love to the point of ignorance, the proverb encourages individuals to exercise caution and awareness in their romantic endeavors. It serves as a reminder that love should not cloud one's judgment or lead them to overlook warning signs or red flags in a relationship.

It also offers valuable advice on maintaining a healthy balance in relationships and avoiding the pitfalls of being overly infatuated. It encourages individuals to approach love with mindfulness and discernment, thereby safeguarding themselves from potential heartache or disappointment. By heeding the wisdom contained in this proverb, people can cultivate greater self-awareness and emotional resilience in their romantic pursuits.

By acknowledging the presence of "rain," the proverb underscores the importance of resilience and adaptability in navigating life's challenges. Love, while a source of joy and fulfillment, does not shield us from adversity. Instead, it is our ability to recognize and respond to difficulties that ultimately strengthens the bonds of love and deepens our connection with others.

Embedded within the proverb is an invitation to cultivate self-awareness and introspection. It encourages individuals to examine their emotions, motivations, and perceptions with honesty and clarity. By maintaining a conscious awareness of both the joys and trials of love, we can cultivate greater insight into ourselves and our relationships.

Mark Irabor

The proverb offers valuable insights for individuals navigating the complexities of romantic love, friendship, and familial bonds. It advises on balancing passion and pragmatism. In romantic relationships, the initial stages of infatuation can often obscure the realities of compatibility, communication, and shared values. The proverb reminds us to temper the intensity of our emotions with a pragmatic assessment of the relationship's dynamics. By cultivating open communication and mutual respect, couples can weather the storms of life together with greater resilience and understanding.

In addition, the proverb advises that love should enhance our sense of self and autonomy rather than diminish it. The proverb encourages individuals to maintain a healthy sense of self-awareness and independence within their relationships. Respecting boundaries, both emotional and physical, fosters a sense of trust and mutual respect that is essential for the long-term health and sustainability of any partnership.

The proverb offers valuable advice on maintaining a healthy balance in relationships and avoiding the pitfalls of being overly infatuated. It encourages individuals to approach love with mindfulness and discernment, thereby safeguarding themselves from potential heartache or disappointment. By heeding the wisdom contained in this proverb, people can cultivate greater self-awareness and emotional resilience in their romantic pursuits.

Looking ahead, the proverb is likely to continue resonating with audiences and offering valuable insights into the complexities of human relationships. As Nigerian culture evolves and adapts to changing societal norms, this timeless wisdom will remain a source of guidance and inspiration for generations to come. By reflecting on the lessons embedded in this proverb, individuals can navigate the challenges of love with greater wisdom and discernment, ultimately fostering healthier and more fulfilling connections.

The proverb also embraces vulnerability and growth since love requires vulnerability—the willingness to open oneself up to joy, but also to the possibility of pain. The proverb invites us to embrace the full spectrum of human experience, recognizing that growth often emerges from adversity. By confronting challenges together with courage and compassion, couples can deepen their bond and forge a more resilient partnership.

While the proverb is often associated with romantic love, its wisdom transcends the confines of any single relationship or context. It speaks to the broader human experience, encompassing themes of resilience, empathy, and interconnectedness.

In friendships and community bonds, the proverb encourages empathy and solidarity in times of adversity. True companionship is not solely defined by shared moments of joy but by the willingness to stand by one another through life's trials. By fostering a sense of mutual support and understanding, friendships can weather the storms of life with grace and resilience.

The wisdom of the proverb reflects universal truths that resonate across cultures and societies. In an increasingly interconnected world, the challenges we face—from social injustice to environmental crises—demand collective action and empathy. By embracing the wisdom of the proverb, we can cultivate a deeper sense of empathy and solidarity that transcends geographical and cultural boundaries.

In the embroidery of human experience, love serves as both a beacon of hope and a mirror to our deepest vulnerabilities. This proverb offers a timeless reminder of the importance of maintaining perspective, resilience, and empathy in the face of life's challenges. Whether in matters of the heart, friendships, or global solidarity, the wisdom captured within this proverb invites us to navigate the complexities of love and reality with clarity, courage, and compassion. As we embrace the duality of love—the ecstasy and the adversity—we discover the true depth of our humanity and our capacity for growth and connection.

Before the Dance

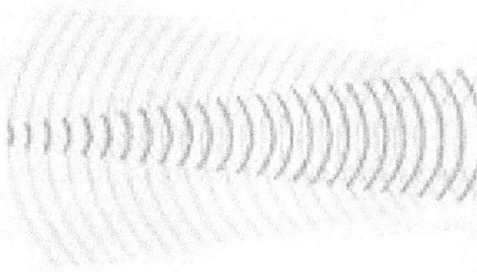

"Before you go out with a widow,
you must first ask what killed her husband."
~African Proverb

This proverb serves as a guiding principle in matters of the heart, offering timeless wisdom that transcends generations and borders. At its core, it emphasizes the necessity of seeking understanding and empathy before entering into a romantic relationship, especially with someone who has experienced loss.

To fully grasp the depth of this proverb, one must delve into its layers of meaning and implications. On the surface, it appears to be a practical piece of advice, urging individuals to inquire about the circumstances surrounding the death of a widow's husband before pursuing a romantic connection however, beneath this practicality lies a deeper message about empathy, compassion, and the acknowledgment of past traumas.

The death of a spouse is not only a personal loss but also a communal event, with implications that extend far beyond the individual. By asking about the circumstances of the husband's death, one demonstrates sensitivity to the widow's experience and acknowledges the significance of her past in shaping her present.

Besides, the proverb highlights the importance of communication and transparency in relationships. Inquiring about the widow's past demonstrates a willingness to engage in open and honest dialogue, laying the foundation for trust and understanding to flourish. It serves as a reminder that meaningful connections are built on a bedrock of mutual respect and vulnerability.

Furthermore, the proverb underscores the broader theme of empathy and compassion. By encouraging individuals to consider the widow's experiences and emotions, it promotes a culture of empathy and solidarity, where community members support and uplift each other in times of need. In doing so, it fosters a sense of interconnectedness and belonging within the community.

Beyond its cultural significance, the proverb holds universal relevance, offering insights that resonate across different societies and contexts. Regardless of cultural background, the idea of seeking understanding and empathy before entering into a relationship is universally applicable. In a world where relationships are often marred by misunderstandings and conflicts, the wisdom embedded within this proverb serves as a timeless reminder of the importance of empathy and compassion in fostering meaningful connections.

Also, the proverb speaks to the broader issue of how society treats widows and individuals who have experienced loss. In many cultures, widows face stigma, discrimination, and social isolation, making it even more crucial to approach them with empathy and understanding. By asking about the widow's past, one acknowledges her experiences and validates her grief, offering a sense of solace and support in a time of need. Nonetheless, the proverb sends the message that if the husband died of a mysterious circumstance… stay away!

In a modern context, where dating and relationships are often characterized by superficiality and instant gratification, the wisdom of this proverb takes on added significance. It challenges individuals to move beyond surface-level interactions and to engage with each other on a deeper level, where vulnerabilities are shared, and true connections are forged. In a society that often values appearance over substance, the proverb serves as a tender reminder of the importance of authenticity and sincerity in relationships.

Likewise, the proverb encourages reflection and self-awareness, prompting individuals to reflect on their own motivations and intentions before pursuing a romantic connection. By asking about the widow's past, one is forced to confront their own biases and prejudices, as well as their capacity for empathy and compassion. In doing so, it invites a deeper understanding of oneself and others, fostering personal growth and emotional maturity.

The proverb offers profound insights into the complexities of relationships and the importance of understanding and empathy. It serves as a timeless reminder of the significance of acknowledging and honoring each other's pasts, as well as the power of open and honest communication in fostering meaningful connections. In a world that often values superficiality and instant gratification, the wisdom of this proverb is more relevant than ever, challenging individuals to move beyond surface-level interactions and to engage with each other on a deeper, more meaningful level.

The Legacy of Thorns

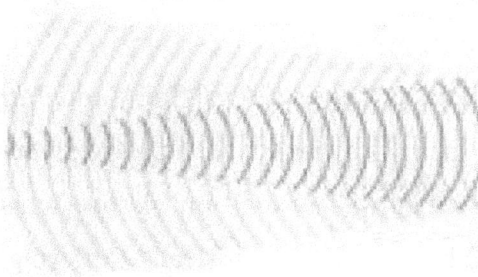

"Never plant thorns on someone's path. Your children may take that route barefooted one day."
~African Proverb

That's a profound proverb emphasizing the importance of kindness and compassion in our actions toward others. It's a reminder that the consequences of our actions can extend beyond our own lives and affect future generations. It underscores the interconnectedness of humanity and the importance of considering how our choices today may impact those who come after us.

In a small village of Abeokuta in Ogun State, Nigeria, there lived a man named Taye. Taye was known throughout the village for his sharp tongue and quick temper. He would often speak harshly to his neighbors, criticizing their actions and spreading gossip wherever he went. Despite his abrasive demeanor, Taye was a skilled farmer, tending to his fields with care and dedication.

One day, as Taye was walking through the village, he passed by a young boy named Majid. Majid was struggling to carry a heavy load of firewood on his back, his small frame barely able to bear the weight. Instead of offering to help, Taye scoffed at Majid and muttered under his breath about the laziness of the younger generation.

As the years passed, Taye's reputation for cruelty only grew. He would take pleasure in mocking others and causing strife wherever he went. Despite the pleas of his wife and children to change his ways, Taye remained stubborn and unyielding, convinced of his own superiority.

Meanwhile, Majid grew into a kind and compassionate young man, beloved by all who knew him. He would often spend his free time helping the elderly, fetching water for his neighbors, and volunteering at the village school. His acts of kindness endeared him to the entire community, and he became known as the village's shining light.

One day, disaster struck the village. A severe drought swept through the land, causing crops to wither and streams to dry up. Families began to go hungry, and desperation spread like wildfire. In the midst of the chaos, Taye found himself facing the consequences of his actions.

With his fields barren and his livelihood in jeopardy, Taje turned to his neighbors for help. But instead of helping, they turned him away, remembering all the times he had scorned and belittled them in the past. Desperate and alone, Taye realized the extent of the thorns he had planted on his own path.

Meanwhile, Majid sprang into action, organizing relief efforts and rallying the villagers together in their time of need. He distributed food and water to those most affected by the drought, offering words of comfort and encouragement along the way. Despite his own struggles, Majid remained steadfast in his commitment to helping others, embodying the true spirit of compassion and empathy.

As the days turned into weeks and the drought showed no signs of abating, Taye's situation grew increasingly dire. With no one to turn to and no hope in sight, he found himself on the brink of despair. It was then that Majid approached him, offering a hand of friendship and forgiveness.

"I know we haven't always seen eye to eye, but we are all struggling in our own ways," Majid said, his voice filled with sincerity. "Let us put aside our differences and come together as one community to overcome this challenge."

Moved by Majid's generosity and grace, Taye felt a sting of remorse for the pain he had caused others over the years. With tears in his eyes, he accepted Majid's offer of reconciliation and joined forces with his neighbors to weather the storm.

As the villagers worked side by side, their bonds grew stronger, and they emerged from the drought more resilient than ever before. Though the scars of the past lingered, they served as a reminder of the importance of kindness and compassion in the face of adversity.

Years later, as Taye sat beneath the shade of a towering baobab tree, watching his grandchildren play in the distance, he reflected on the lessons he had learned. He realized that true wealth was not measured in material possessions or worldly success, but in the relationships, we build and the impact we have on others.

And as he looked upon the smiling faces of his loved ones, Taye vowed to never again plant thorns on someone's path, knowing that his children and grandchildren may one day walk that same road barefooted. For he had learned that true happiness lies in lifting others up, rather than tearing them down.

Love and the Marketplace

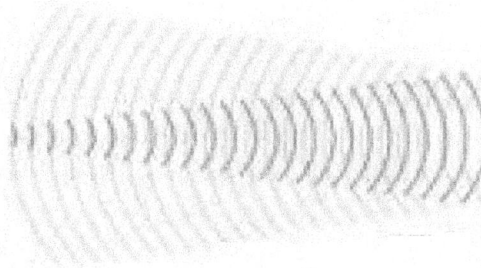

*"A marketplace is not a place for
husband and wife to argue."*
~Nigerian Proverb

The marketplace is not just a place to buy and sell goods but
also a social hub where people gather to catch up with friends,
exchange news, and even engage in friendly banter. However,

the proverb serves as a reminder that there are certain conversations and behaviors that are not appropriate in public settings.

The marketplace is a place of commerce and community where people come together to engage in business and social interactions. It is a public space where people from all walks of life converge, and it is important to maintain a sense of decorum and respect for others. Arguing with a spouse in a marketplace can disrupt the peace and harmony of the environment and can make others feel uncomfortable or even unsafe.

Couples may have disagreements and arguments from time to time, but it is important to remember that there is a time and a place for everything. The marketplace is not the appropriate setting for airing personal grievances or engaging in heated debates. It is a place where people come to conduct business and socialize, and bringing personal conflicts into this public space can be disruptive and inappropriate.

Moreover, arguing in public, especially in a marketplace, can also be seen as a sign of disrespect towards one's spouse. It can create a negative perception of the relationship and can undermine the bond of trust and respect between partners. It is important for couples to address their conflicts in a private and respectful manner, where they can have open and honest conversations without the prying eyes and ears of strangers.

To conclude, this African proverb, "A marketplace is not a place for a husband and wife to argue" reminds us of the importance of maintaining decorum and respect in public spaces. While it is natural for couples to have disagreements, it is crucial to choose the appropriate time and place to address these issues. By showing respect for one another and for the community around them, couples can strengthen their relationship and contribute to the peace and harmony of the society in which they live.

The Priest and the Storm

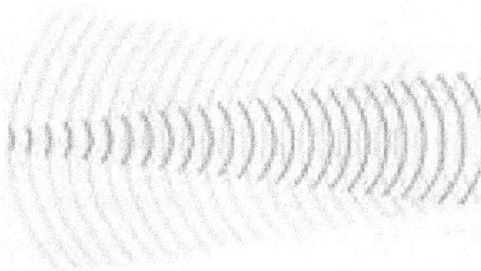

"A priest who invokes a storm on his people cannot prevent his house from destruction."
~Nigerian Proverb

This proverb carries a powerful message about the consequences of one's actions, particularly those in positions of authority or leadership. It suggests that leaders who bring harm to their own community or followers cannot escape the repercussions, even if they try to protect themselves or their own interests.

The proverb highlights the interrelation of individuals within a community and the importance of responsible leadership. That those in positions of influence and power have a responsibility to act in the best interest of their community, as their actions can have far-reaching repercussions. Their role was to guide and protect the people, both spiritually and physically.

However, if a priest were to use their powers to harm instead of help, they would ultimately bring destruction upon themselves and their own household. The symbol of invoking a storm on his people highlights the destructive power that a leader can wield if they chooses to act in a selfish or malevolent manner. Just as a storm can cause widespread devastation and chaos, so can a leader's actions have a harmful impact on those under their care.

The consequences of such actions are not limited to the immediate victims but can extend to the perpetrators themselves, resulting in the destruction of their own houses. This proverb serves as a reminder that those in positions of authority must exercise their power with wisdom and integrity.

Leaders have a duty to act in the best interest of their

community, promoting harmony and well-being rather than discord and destruction. By abusing their power or acting selfishly, they not only harm others but also bring about their own downfall.

This proverb remains relevant as a cautionary tale to leaders in all walks of life. Whether in politics, business, or religion, those in positions of influence must consider the long-term consequences of their actions. It is only by acting with compassion, honesty, and foresight that they can truly protect and preserve their own house.

The lesson of this proverb is clear: to sow destruction is to reap destruction, and true leadership requires a commitment to the well-being of all.

Envy's Shadow

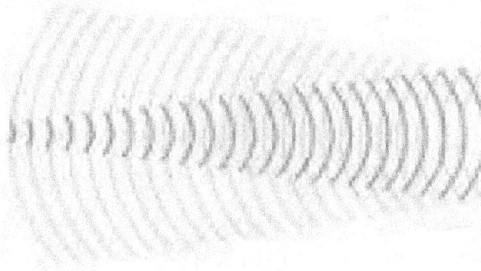

"Do not be surprised by haters they have seen your success."
~African Proverb

Success is something that many people aspire to achieve in their lives. It brings with it a sense of fulfillment, pride, and accomplishment. However, success also has a dark side that should not be ignored.

Throughout history, individuals who have achieved great success have always been met with criticism and negativity from others. However, this proverb speaks to the idea that when you are successful and doing well for yourself, there will always be people who try to bring you down out of jealousy or insecurity.

In today's highly connected world, with social media and the internet, it is easier than ever for people to voice their opinions and spread negativity. As a result, it is common to see successful individuals facing backlash and criticism from strangers who have never even met them. This can be disheartening and frustrating, but it is important to remember that this criticism often comes from a place of envy.

When someone is successful, it can trigger feelings of inadequacy in others who have not achieved the same level of success. Instead of celebrating the accomplishments of others, these individuals may try to tear them down in order to make themselves feel better. This behavior is toxic and serves no purpose other than to bring others down.

It is crucial for successful individuals to not let the negativity of haters affect them. Instead of being surprised or discouraged by these individuals, it is important to remember that their criticism reflects their own insecurities and inadequacies. By staying focused on their goals and continuing to work hard, successful individuals can rise above the noise and prove their critics wrong.

To sum up, do not let the negativity of others bring you down. When you are successful, there will always be people who try to diminish your accomplishments out of jealousy. Instead of letting this criticism affect you, use it as motivation to continue striving for greatness. Stay focused on your goals and surround yourself with positive, supportive individuals who celebrate your success rather than tearing you down.

Unveiling Character

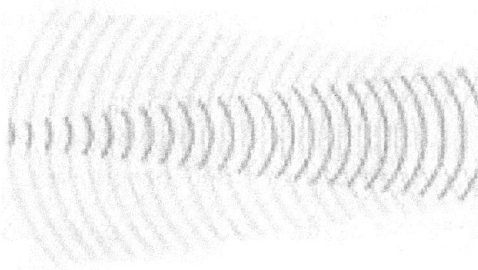

"Everyone will show you who they are;
just give them time."
~Nigerian Proverb

The proverb emphasizes the importance of being patient and observant to understand someone's character truly. Oftentimes, people may put on a facade or hide their true selves, but eventually, their true colors will reveal themselves through their actions and behavior.

In today's fast-paced world, making quick judgments about others can be easy based on surface-level interactions or appearances. However, this proverb serves as a reminder to not jump to conclusions and instead take the time to get to know someone before forming an opinion about them.

Through spending time with someone, listening to them, and observing how they engage with others, we can truly understand who they are as a person. People may try to hide their true selves for various reasons - fear of judgment, past experiences, or insecurities - but given enough time, their true nature will shine through.

By practicing patience and observation, we can steer clear of making hasty assumptions about others. Instead, we can develop a more genuine and accurate understanding of who they are. This paves the way for authentic relationships built on trust and mutual respect, enriching our lives in ways we might not have imagined.

Lastly, the proverb imparts a valuable lesson. It underscores the significance of patience and understanding in our quest to know others. By allowing people the time and space to be themselves, we can forge deeper connections and nurture more meaningful relationships.

The Unforgettable Gaze

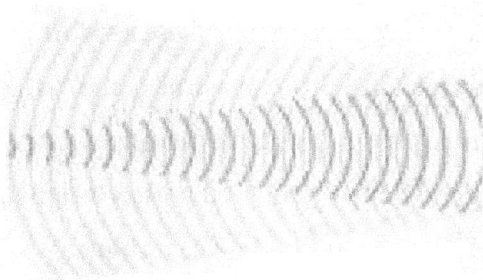

"The eye never forgets what the heart has seen."
~African Proverb

There once was a young girl named Nala who lived in a small village in East Africa. Nala had a special gift - she could see things others could not. Her eyes were like windows to her soul, reflecting the beauty and pain of the world around her.

From a young age, Nala was drawn to the natural beauty of her village. She would spend hours wandering through the lush forests, marveling at the vibrant colors of the flowers and the melodious songs of the birds. But Nala's gift also allowed her to see the darker side of life.

She witnessed the suffering of her people, the poverty, and the injustice that plagued her village. Despite the hardships she faced, Nala's resilience shone through. She believed her gift was a blessing, a reminder that beauty existed even in the darkest times. She drew strength from the love and resilience of her people, and her heart swelled with compassion for those less fortunate.

A devastating drought struck the village one day, leaving the crops withered and the people hungry. Nala watched as her friends and family struggled to survive, their faces etched with pain and despair. But instead of turning away, Nala opened her heart and offered a helping hand to those in need. She worked tirelessly, gathering whatever resources she could find and distributing them among the villagers. She comforted the sick and the elderly, offering them words of solace and hope. And as she looked into their eyes, she could see the gratitude and strength that dwelled within their hearts.

Despite their hardships, Nala and her people found

solace in each other's company. They shared their stories and laughter, finding joy in life's simple pleasures. Through it all, Nala's eyes never forgot the pain and suffering she had witnessed, but her heart never lost sight of the love and resilience that defined her village.

As the drought finally ended, the town emerged more robust and more united than ever before. The crops flourished, the people thrived, and Nala's gift shone like a beacon of light in the darkness. As she looked around at the smiling faces of her people, she realized that the eye never forgets what the heart has seen - but it also never loses sight of the beauty and hope that resides within us all.

The proverb illustrates the interconnectedness of our emotions and perceptions, suggesting that our hearts serve as emotional filters that shape our understanding and recollection of the world around us.

When we experience something intensely emotional, whether joy, sorrow, pain, or love, it can leave a lasting imprint on our hearts and minds; our emotions color our perceptions and interpretations of events, influencing how we remember them. This is why some memories are vivid and memorable while others fade away. As the proverb suggests, the eye is the window through which we see the world around us. But the heart gives meaning and significance to what we see. Our emotional responses to the events we witness can etch them into our memories, ensuring they are not easily forgotten.

The idea that the eye never forgets what the heart has seen also speaks to the interconnectedness of our emotions and memories. Our emotional responses to events can trigger strong memories that stay with us long after the events have passed. This is why certain sights, sounds, and smells can evoke powerful emotions and memories from our past.

Ultimately, this proverb reminds us of the importance of acknowledging and honoring our feelings in how we perceive and remember the world around us. By recognizing our hearts' impact on our memories, we can better understand ourselves and the experiences that shape us. This understanding empowers us to navigate life's challenges with resilience.

Love's Unpredictable Shower

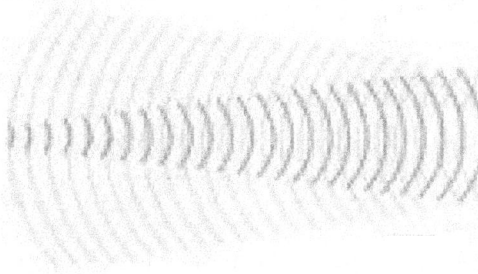

*"Love is like rain; it does not choose
the grass on which it falls."*
~African Proverb

Love is a universal emotion that transcends all boundaries and exists in every corner of the world. One African proverb beautifully captures love's essence: "Love is like rain; it does not choose the grass on which it falls." This proverb signifies that love is unconditional and unbiased; it simply flows freely and abundantly, touching everything in its path.

Like rain, love does not discriminate based on who or what it falls upon. It does not favor one person over another or select a specific type of individual to bestow its blessings upon. Love is a force of nature that showers warmth and kindness upon all without prejudice or judgment.

This proverb teaches us an important lesson about love – that it is a powerful and profound force that has the ability to bring people together, regardless of their differences. Love has the capacity to bridge gaps, heal wounds, and create unity among individuals from all walks of life.

In a world that is often divided by hate, anger, and conflict, the message behind this African proverb is more relevant than ever. It reminds us that love is the antidote to all negativity and animosity and that we can create a more compassionate and harmonious society by embracing love in all its forms.

So, let us all strive to be like the rain – to shower love upon everyone we meet without discrimination or bias. Let us be the catalyst for change, the bringers of peace and understanding, and the bearers of love in a world that desperately needs it. For love is indeed like rain, and it is up to us to spread its beauty and power far and wide.

"For the Lord giveth wisdom: out of His mouth cometh knowledge and understanding."

Proverbs 2:6 (KJV)

Also by Mark Irabor

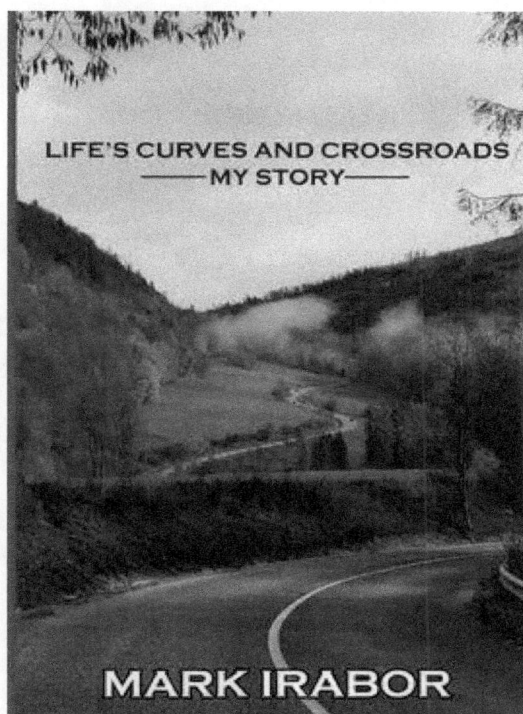

LIFE'S CURVES AND CROSSROADS
——MY STORY——

MARK IRABOR